The Eighth House

The Eighth House

A murder, a mother, a haunting

Written by Linda Segtnan
Translated by Elizabeth
Clark Wessel

ITHAKA

First published in the UK by Ithaka Press
An imprint of Black & White Publishing Group
A Bonnier Books UK company

4th Floor, Victoria House,
Bloomsbury Square,
London, WC1B 4DA

Owned by Bonnier Books
Sveavägen 56, Stockholm, Sweden

Hardback — 978-1-80418-431-8
Trade Paperback — 978-1-80418-574-2
Ebook — 978-1-80418-512-4

A CIP catalogue of this book is available from the British Library.

Typeset by IDSUK (Data Connection) Ltd
Printed and bound by Clays Ltd, Elcograf S.p.A.

1 3 5 7 9 10 8 6 4 2

Every reasonable effort has been made to trace copyright holders of material
reproduced in this book, but if any have been inadvertently overlooked the
publishers would be glad to hear from them.

Ithaka Press is an imprint of Bonnier Books UK
www.bonnierbooks.co.uk

For Sam and Vivianne

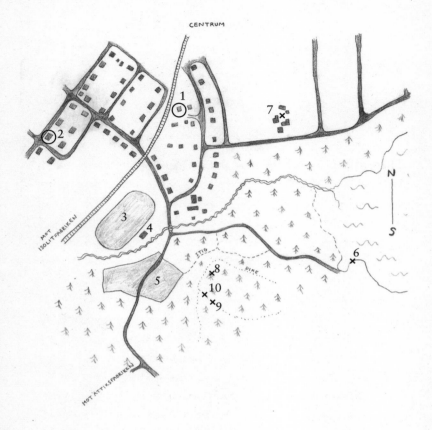

1. The Sivander residence
2. The Sommer residence
3. The new football field
4. The changing rooms
5. The old football field
6. The junkyard
7. The approximate location of Elin Söberg's farm
8. The spot where Birgitta Sivander's clogs are found
9. Where the tracks in the ditch start
10. Where Birgitta is found

There is a place where it is always dark, where earth wields another kind of gravity. Summer will never come here again. The ground is covered in wet, disintegrating leaves. A ring of spruces rises high above, like a menacing crowd. They stoop over me while I search for you. They grant no opening, let in no light. My daughter and I are dragged inexorably towards the cold earth; we slip on old leaves. I shelter her with my body, hold her deep inside of me so she won't see, won't feel the chill. A sister to her in a sense, or a sister to me, pulls us deeper into the woods. I search on, rain pounding against my head, and I want to go home. My abdomen contracts again and again. My daughter moves anxiously inside my pelvis, while I, legs splayed wide, slowly and heavily drag our bodies forward one foot at a time. From my heart to a place deeper in this forest runs a thread of yarn. It's drawn taut. But I don't know that – I want to give up and lie down.

That is when I hear a voice:

Here it is.

The words are coming from my own mouth, but they're not my words. *Here it is.* I hear it over and over again. Ahead of me, I see a place marked with a white circle. I am drawn closer and I realise those are white feathers. Beside them is the ditch. Here it is. I found you.

GIRL FLED BAREFOOT, STRUGGLED TO SURVIVE

Police in southern Sweden are still conducting an exhaustive search for a suspect in the brutal slaying of 9-year-old Perstorp native, Birgitta Sivander. [. . .] The autopsy, performed on Saturday afternoon at Hässleholm hospital by Professor Einar Sjöwall, revealed the cause of death was blunt force trauma to the head. No signs of rape were detected during the autopsy. However, the homicide squad has concluded that the young girl was lured into the forest by an abnormal individual [. . .]

Birgitta Sivander, daughter of engineer Valdemar Sivander at Perstorp's acetum factory, disappeared at approximately 8pm on Friday. She'd spent the evening at the football field watching practice. Several young players observed her. She was last seen leaving the field in the direction of her home.

The murdered girl, 9-year-old Birgitta Sivander, Perstorp

I first visited the National Library of Sweden nearly twenty years ago, while studying bookbinding. We went there on a study trip, to a tiny room many floors beneath the ground. There, behind a door several decimetres thick, the library kept its most rare and valuable books. An archivist in white cotton gloves showed us a manuscript painstakingly written and bound by a monk, which contained secret, obscene images only visible when you bent the front section. Another book was bound in human skin.

A few years later, while studying for my bachelor's degree in history, I'd go to that library several times a week. At first I sat in the large reading room with the other students. But despite the high ceiling and large windows, the air there was always stuffy. While writing my thesis, I was pregnant with Sam and terrified of getting sick. That's when I started taking the elevator down to the Microfilm Reading Room, five floors underground.

After finishing at the university, I began working as a researcher for historical walking tours, and made that reading room my office. It's quiet there, except when the reels are being wound. The ceiling, low and grey, is lit with fluorescent lamps. Oversized computer screens shine on desks, separated by plywood boards. You can use them to read digitised newspapers. They radiate heat. After a few hours of reading, my face feels sunburned.

At the back of the room stand the old microfilm readers. The microfilmed newspapers are stored in the grey filing cabinets running along the left side of the room. Cold light falls on hunched shoulders and rounded necks. In one corner, an elderly man always sat sleeping.

The seed is sown on a spring day in 2018. I'm working on a new commission for a historical tour, skimming through scanned pages of yellowed newspapers, noting a headline here and there. Nothing fits. I place snus beneath my lip and keep searching, until I stumble onto a small news item from 1948. At first, I dismiss it as irrelevant.

But before I click forward, my gaze is caught by the image of a young girl. Her eyes, as deep as wells, stare out at me from a grainy picture. A smile plays at the corner of her mouth. Her face is so difficult to interpret. It changes all the time. One moment I think she looks unsure, the next mildly amused. Then I read the thick, black headline above and realise Birgitta Sivander never grew any older than she was in this picture – she was murdered. Her life was stolen from her, not in the city I am writing the historical tour about, but in Perstorp, in Skåne, in the south of Sweden.

A flash burns in my chest. Ever since Sam was born, like many new parents, I've become more sensitive to the suffering of children. I try to avoid it, but something in that young girl's gaze compels me. I push my face towards the screen, inspecting the photo more closely, and my chair creaks loudly.

This is the moment of conception; this is when an obsession takes root in my belly.

I'm still at the National Library reading article after article. I forget about my hunger and the time. For hours, I sit trans-fixed, while dinner grows cold on our kitchen table at home and my son starts asking where his mother is. By the time I get home, he's already asleep. I lie awake all night trying to fit it together. The murder remains unsolved. Like a question with no answer, it's been met with uncomfortable silence for more than seventy years, while a killer has gone free. Why murder a 9-year-old girl? She wasn't raped. Rape is the only motive I know of for the murder of little girls, unless the killer is a close relative.

The story grabs on to something inside me. Something recognisable, some paralysing fear. I've heard it said the person you end up having children with after 30 is just a matter of chance. That it's less about finding a soulmate, and more about meeting at the right age and in the right circumstances. Maybe that's the case for me and Birgitta, too. At that particular moment in the archive, I am susceptible to her gaze and her fate, and it gives new strength to fears that already had me in their stranglehold.

Still, it's unfair to think of her in that way. I can't completely let go of the idea that we might have known each other. Perhaps we crossed paths in a previous life. She could have been my child. Or maybe we were meant to meet when she was an old woman and I, a young one.

For days after my visit to the National Library, I can hear her hurried footsteps in the mud behind me, on my way to the subway, on my way to preschool. I close my eyes and urge her to run faster, while also trying to convince her to turn around. I *need* to see who's chasing her. I imagine myself as an enormous bird that can grab her by the arms with my talons and lift her away. I watch her killer getting smaller and smaller.

I place her on the ground outside her front door, and she runs inside shouting, 'Mama! Mama! You'll never guess what happened!'

But none of it is real. She didn't run fast enough. She never got home.

Between my city tours and after putting Sam to bed, I begin to write. It's jumbled and formless, but the story needs a place to go. Justus asks me what I'm working on. Family and friends do, too. I have a hard time explaining to them why I have no time to meet up or do pickup at preschool or take on new paid assignments. I tell them, vaguely, that I have to write. When they ask me what about, I answer: *a murder*. Oh, that's exciting, they say. It turns my stomach. So, I clarify: *I'm writing about the murder of a little girl*. Oh no, that's terrible!

And then they fall into two groups – those who don't want to know any more about it, and those who lean forward and say, tell me more.

In a parallel reality to my own, she's still riding a bike. My present and hers have begun to run beside each other. A god with a jug in each hand pours water into a silver bowl. Time flows. It glitters in the sun. Both hers and mine, and eventually we will meet. I imagine myself as a 9-year-old. A bell tolls inside me for her. It's a Friday, a warm day in May. She's gone to pick flowers. Cotton-grass.

She lies in the grass with her face in the sun. She can hear the long whistle of a train echo across the fields. She's biked five kilometres from home, even though she's not supposed to go so far. She is going to die soon. But somewhere she's still on her bike, still lying among the cotton-grass, its soft flowers caressing her.

Part One
Budding Flower

A sick god dwells
in these gloomy woods.
In the dim woods the blossoms are pale
and the birds bashful.
Why is the wind whispering warnings
and the way dark with foreboding?
In shadows, there lies a sick god
dreaming evil dreams . . .

Edith Södergran, 'Forest Darkness'

Birgitta's story begins one summer day in 1935 with two young people on a bright, sandy beach. I go closer. This scene is set in Hanko, Finland. The water is black, and the sand reflects the Milky Way. There is Margit Bratt. She's distinct; even from a distance it's clear she's not just anyone. Her posture is proud, her gestures smooth, her face shaped like an oval mirror. This is the last night General Mannerheim's café, the House of the Four Winds, will be open this summer. There's a huge slide you can ride straight into the sea.

Margit is here with her parents and sister. She's attending ballet school and lives in a large apartment in the part of Stockholm where the Åhléns City department store stands today. They're considered a fine family, the Bratts. Across from them, not far from a roving Margit, stands a young civil engineer named Valdemar Sivander. He's beautiful, his body poetically graceful. The Sivander family aren't considered quite so fine as the Bratts, but Margit is too young to care.

The waves roll in quietly towards the land, and the sound of voices and laughter can be heard in the distance. Margit's parents will soon start to wonder where she is. In Stockholm, a more suitable match awaits her, a young man with connections to the royal family. But fate has something else in mind, and a low flame had been lit inside Margit earlier that day as she met Valdemar's eyes, above the bathers and beneath a sunny sky.

When will they kiss for the first time? Surely it won't be long; the engagement will be announced as early as June of that summer. They'll be married in St Stephen's church on

20 May of the following year. By then Margit will be carrying a child in her womb. The baby will be born on 1 December. The birth will be a long and difficult one. It is Birgitta's big brother Karl who arrives first. Birgitta is still waiting.

When my son, Sam, was little, he told me that before he arrived in my belly, he lived in space with his cousin Maya, waiting to come to us. Similarly, Birgitta floats above the house on Varvsgatan, watching as her screaming brother comes into the world at the maternity hospital Pro Patria.

Soon their little family will pack up their apartment on Södermalm and move out to Hässelby, a suburb north-west of the city. There, an avenue leads to a large, bright building. The grand house, called Riddersvik, rises proudly at its end. Valdemar's parents live there and they allow their son and his family to move in on the upper floor. Two pillars stand on either side of the doors and above the entrance is written *Anno MDCCLXII*. There is a stone staircase furrowed by thousands of footsteps over the centuries.

This is where Birgitta will land on earth, as 1937 turns to 1938. This time, Margit walks around in large rooms with high ceilings, over creaking floor tiles, as her belly grows. Birgitta arrives in late summer.

I stop here to remember what it feels like to give birth to a child. I can still remember the impossibly steep mountain peak, right before the last contraction pushed my pelvis open. A small figure slid out like a seal. Little bodies, still warm from the womb, exit into the cold, are exposed to bright light and sharp sounds. When Birgitta arrived naked in the world, fathers weren't allowed to be present, and babies weren't laid onto bare breasts. They were swaddled, weighed and measured. And then they were left alone. But I find it difficult to think about that. So I transform it in my mind; the tiny baby is lifted and then laid atop a beating heart.

Once, I was pregnant and lost the baby. I remember standing in a meadow in Vinterviken not knowing how to get home. Justus had to come pick me up. I went to the Prima psychiatry clinic and told them I might want to die. I thought they'd finally give me some help. But I was denied. I went home again. I don't remember much from this time.

Three years later I had my tarot read. The reader formulated her words carefully, but I knew what she meant to say – we were going to have another child. She didn't know we were already trying. I had an acupuncture appointment once a week. I was boiling Chinese herbs, a mixture of twigs, bits of bark and God knows what else, and pouring it down my throat quickly over the sink every day. I drank two litres of it a week out of pure desperation; it tasted like an ashtray.

When the cards were placed on the table, I drew a Six of Pentacles, Six of Swords and, as my trump card, the Six of Cups – the lovers. 666. The number of the Devil. But the opposite was on its way, a tiny god.

Birgitta was born, like her brother, at the Pro Patria maternity hospital in Stockholm. I eagerly decipher the almost unreadable lines in the baptismal register. It feels like time has stood still here, as though the priest's pen only just left the paper, and Birgitta is still an infant. First, they recorded the birth in the maternity hospital's baptismal register. Child 605, born on 20 August 1938. Father's and mother's name and date of birth. Riddersvik, Hässelby. Birgitta was also entered in the Järfälla parish's baptismal register, as Inger Birgitta. I'm desperate for more. What was the pregnancy like? How did the birth progress? What was Birgitta like as a baby?

Past Riddersvik's pillars and over its threshold, they carried her home for the first time. She slowly acquired a circadian rhythm there, felt the security and warmth of the breast. She cried, was rocked and hushed. Got her first taste of real food and her first tooth. Her body rounded. She started to crawl across those wide tiles. Laughed at her brother.

They will leave this house and Stockholm when she's close to a year old. Valdemar will get a new job in Skellefteå, where the family will stay for two years until they move to Perstorp. In Skellefteå he is the head of a department in a smeltery. Much at the beginning of this story feels cinematic and romantic, but not this part. Molten metal being poured into crucibles like liquid gold is beautiful. But the staff are given inadequate protective equipment, and Valdemar will later develop a cancer whose origin probably came from the lead and arsenic found here. The benefits of this job included a newly built company house, a nanny and a maid.

When Birgitta is 3 years old, a new little brother arrives – Erik is born on Halloween 1941. The family's home sits near the railway, and while the parents are occupied with the new baby, Karl and Birgitta sneak over to the tracks to lay down coins. They hop off before a train passes by. Afterwards, the coins are shiny and flat.

I step off a train in Lund, an hour from Perstorp, into the spring air of early May. A year's gone by since that evening at the National Library, and I have been waiting for permission to access the 1948 police investigation. My days have been filled with fussing over overalls, writing city tours, cooking dinner, playing with Lego. After Sam has gone to sleep, I've discussed the murder with Justus, combing over it repeatedly. At night I've dreamed of Birgitta. Sometimes I have a blurry impression of almost brushing her fingertips, before she slips away into nothingness. Now I'm eager; I almost feel like I'm about to meet her.

My friend Idha meets me at the station and leads me over the cobblestone streets of Lund. In Stockholm I left behind trees in bud, cold lingering in the air. Down here the lilacs are already blooming. Tomorrow morning I plan to take the bus to the archive as soon as it opens. I want the maximum amount of time with the material before they close.

The next day, the archivist tells me that they have arranged for me to have my own room; the contents of the files include pictures that aren't suitable for everyone's eyes. I unwind the string around the files, apprehensive about what I'll see. Will the pictures come now? Or now? Sometimes the copies of interrogations and forensic statements are the kinds made on cheap, semi-transparent paper. Sometimes the pages are stained. Influenced by all the whodunnits I have consumed from an early age, I imagine the detectives drinking strong coffee late at night, exhausted but determined not to give up until they catch the killer. Coffee splashes over the rim of the cup when one stands up too quickly to put a thumbtack in a map. Or write down something on a blackboard. On one page there's a flattened mosquito. It makes my head swim.

Inside my womb, cells have started dividing at a furious rate. An embryo has attached to the wall of my uterus, the seed of a girl. A little sister to my son, who's being dropped off at preschool while I sit here, reading about the murder of a child.

My thoughts wander towards my niece, who will soon be eight. I try to steel myself. My niece Maya. My first baby. Her black, shiny hair. Her body – slender, agile and strong as a willow. Her dark eyes flitting from amusement, to anxiety, to joy, to embarrassment, from one second to the next. Girls of that age.

Finally, the inevitable happens – I get to the photo.

There she is.

In fact, she has already left the body lying on that hard, shiny metal table. I hope so anyway. In the Middle Ages, they believed the soul took three days to leave its dwelling. It receded and returned, like a wave. For those three days, someone watched over the body and windows were left open so the soul would have room to come and go. If a person was murdered, you could ask it who committed the murder.

When not on an autopsy table, Birgitta's body was kept for those three important days in cold storage. I wonder how long she'd been dead when this picture was taken. It's not as horrible as I had feared. She's pretty. Blonde hair reaches her jaw-line. She's not skinny, but slender. She looks like she belongs on a bike, riding down a hill at breakneck speed. She looks like she ran down gravel roads with her friends, like she threw herself onto the kitchen chair to eat cheese sandwiches after a long day of playing, then crawled into a narrow bed with an adventure book in her hand. Her eyebrows are straight, her nose slightly tilted and round at the end. She looks like all the girls I've ever known. Even though she has bruises on her face and her eyes are closed. To my layman's eyes, she doesn't look like she's been subjected to deadly violence. I get the feeling it was *easy* to kill her.

The investigation also includes photos from the crime scene. They show the footprints of a sock-wearing child in a shallow ditch. These create a movie in my head I can't escape. Small feet jump into the ditch and run. They're followed by a person in size 42 athletic shoes from the brand Tretorn. Panting, heart racing inside her tiny chest. Moisture seeping through her socks. Later I see it in front of me, over and over, both awake and asleep. I can feel that damp. The desperation and panic. The tiny hope of escape. And then the fall, down into brown water. She stumbles, or is struck down. Soon after that it's over, and we follow her as she escapes her body, the ditch, the woods, Perstorp.

Perstorp. Dominated by marshes, bogs and forests until recently. The ice sheets left behind poor, sandy, clayey soil. A north-eastern moraine. Always sparsely populated. At the Swedish National Heritage Board, you can read about archaeologists finding an old farm beneath a parking lot there. They haven't found much else, but there is a church that dates back to the 12th century. In my mind's eye I can see the grim, hard-working people of Perstorp attending it over the centuries. Born of acidic soil.

One of the earliest descriptions of human interaction in Perstorp concerns a conflict: pastor Niels Lauritzsenn and assistant rector Erasmus Erasmi lived there in such disharmony 'that it was a shame to speak of it'. This note was made during a bishop's visit in 1623. On that same occasion, the parishioners complained about the pastor, saying he'd banned someone without even speaking to them, that he was quarrelsome and possessed 'infamous vices'. The church was in such disrepair they feared the pulpit might fall on their heads during holy services.

Perstorp remained a farming village until 1875 when a violent disruption took place – the railroad line from Helsingborg to Hässleholm was completed and the Industrial Revolution arrived. The town's spiritual centre moved from the church to the railway station, and an industrialised area grew like a fungus beside it. Its factories needed labourers, and so Perstorp became a city. The first company to make its mark there produced acetum, tar and formaldehyde, among other things. It came to be called the Skåne acetum factory.

By the end of the First World War plastics were being produced there, a first in Scandinavia. The smell of acetum, tar, formalin and plastic hung about the city. The workers swam through its fog. They lived on one side of the city, where whole families shared a single room with a kitchen, while their superiors lived on the other, in fine houses where children had their own rooms and were attended by live-in maids and nannies. All the children attended the same school: Central school. They were classmates, but it was awkward whenever children of the workers and white-collar employees played at each other's homes. There was one place where they, or at least the boys, could all meet on equal terms: the football field.

The war in Europe is burning. It's been going on for the whole of Birgitta's life. She was 18 days old the first time Stockholm went dark and began practising for air raids. A state of war must have felt normal to her. Battles in the distance, ration cards, Hitler on the radio. Birgitta's first winter was cold and so were the subsequent three. They called them the War Winters.

But when the Sivander family disembark at Perstorp, not long after New Year's, 1944, those winters are over. This is just a normal winter for southern Sweden. I imagine them packing their home up in a glittering, snow-covered, starry-skied Skellefteå and stepping out into a muddy, foggy and bare-treed Perstorp. In between, they celebrate Christmas with the children's grandparents in Stockholm. Like a ghost, I hover above them and peek in through the frosted windows of the penthouse apartment. I can see a star hanging in a large, arched window. Waxed wooden floors, expensive rugs, golden-framed mirrors and paintings, and small crescent tables with curved legs. A Christmas feast is set out on the table. Candles shine in the tree. Above the fireplace sits a nativity scene.

Margit is leaning forward in an armchair, speaking quietly to Sigrid, her mother. They both have on high heels and dresses. Margit looks upset, but I can't hear what she's saying. Now Karl and Birgitta come racing in through the double doors. Margit straightens up and her face brightens. Sigrid is afraid that they'll overturn the Christmas tree and candles. The nanny, Cecilia, comes running in behind the bigger children, holding the hand of a toddling Erik. She curtsies quickly before hurrying after them, admonishing them in a loud whisper.

I rewind and pause the scene.

Birgitta's shining, happy face in the midst of the laughter, shouting out, 'Wait for me, Karl!'

A velvet dress in a muted colour with a Peter Pan collar and puffed sleeves. A large bow holds her bangs back on one side of her face. Her blonde hair dances and flies away.

After the turn of the year, they arrive at their new home, a modern two-storey house on Gustavsborgsvägen in Perstorp. The basement holds a secret – it's dedicated to the Home Guard and stocked with weapons and equipment. People enter their home at odd times because of it. Birgitta is 5 years old.

I try to remember being 5 years old, but I can't. Sam is 5. He's learned all of his letters and can sound out words on paper. He likes to try out new words and expressions. Turning and twisting them, weighing them in his mouth like a sommelier. 'Mar-vel-lous.'

After a while, they move to a new house close by. The Sivander family become friends with the Bloms, who live next door, and Karl and Birgitta play with their children – Åke, who is the same age as Karl, Yngve, Birgitta's age, and then Bittie. Birgitta has her own room with a balcony. It shares a wall with Mama and Papa's bedroom. Their nanny lives on the floor below. Who does Birgitta run to if she wakes up, sweating from a nightmare? I try to imagine her in front of me. Does she ever step out onto the balcony late at night when all the others are asleep?

Yes, now I see her. It's St Lucy's Day, 1945. Birgitta is 7 years old. She's lying in her bed, listening to the rain thumping on the roof. Washing away freshly fallen snow. She's thinking about that morning.

The nanny, Cecilia, dressed them early, in her room beside the kitchen. It was still dark outside. They were getting ready for the Lucia procession. Erik didn't want to be part of it. Birgitta was playing Lucia with a candle in her hand. Karl was one of the Wise Men, his cotton beard glued on with a paste of flour and water. They crept up the stairs to Mama and Papa's bedroom, holding their costumes in one hand and their candles in the other. About halfway there, Mama called down to say that Erik had changed his mind and wanted to join them. Cecilia pushed past the children and ran up the stairs to get him. Birgitta and Karl stood in silence and waited. Suddenly Birgitta heard a strange sound behind her, and the wall of the stairwell was lit by a rapidly spreading flame. She turned and saw Karl was on fire, his beard burning. The flames were reflected in his wide eyes.

Birgitta is thinking about that right now, while Karl lies alone in a hospital with his hands and feet bound with ropes to keep him from touching his own burned skin.

It's a Friday, the day after Ascension Day in May. Birgitta is 9 years old. In addition to her big brother Karl and little brother Erik, she now has a sister, too – baby Eva, born a few days before Birgitta's ninth birthday.

When Birgitta heard the baby was a girl, she said: 'Will she replace me now?'

But if she feels pushed aside, she never takes it out on Eva. She loves that child, hugging and kissing her as often as she can. This morning, Mama and Papa are going away for the day. A tumult arises in the hallway as they put on their jackets and shoes at the same time as Karl, who's in a hurry to get to school. He laces up his shoes, throws his schoolbag onto his back, shouts a sunny 'Goodbye!', then opens the door and takes the front steps in one hop. Valdemar grabs his hat and Margit pulls on her coat.

'Cecilia, tell Birgitta she'll be late if she doesn't hurry,' Margit calls out.

The nanny rushes down the stairs with Eva in her arms.

'Birgitta says she has a stomach-ache.'

Margit sighs. She has no time for this right now.

'Well then, I suppose she can stay home.'

Eva starts to protest loudly when she realises her parents are leaving. They wave as they rush out the door, offering up a tangle of promises to be back soon. They can hear her heartbreaking cries all the way to the car.

Upstairs, Birgitta is lying in bed, listening to the same scene. She sighs in relief as the car starts and its wheels crackle over gravel. Soon Eva stops crying, and the house falls silent. Birgitta puts her hands over her stomach. It does hurt, right? Sometimes it's hard to really know. Maybe she invented the feeling to avoid school. Maybe school *makes* her stomach ache. Anyway, she doesn't stay home because it's fun. There's nothing to do but pull the blanket over her head, turn her face to the wall and fall back asleep.

A couple of hours later, she gets up and gets dressed. A white slip. Knee socks. A small chequered dress in a multitude of colours. A blue wool cardigan that itches a bit. She can't wait for summer when she doesn't have to wear it anymore. The sun is shining promisingly through the windows, sketching a golden pattern across the wall. When Birgitta enters the kitchen, Cecilia is feeding Eva.

'What are you doing up?' Cecilia asks reproachfully.

Eva smiles widely, and Birgitta makes a face and puts her arms around her while avoiding her messy little hands.

'I feel fine now,' she says. 'Can I go out?'

Cecilia stares at her suspiciously, and then shrugs. After all, it's not her child. Not her job to raise her right.

'What are you planning to do?'

'I thought I'd ride my bike. Go pick some flowers.'

With a sense of freedom expanding in her chest, Birgitta heads out. The thought of all the other kids stuck in a dusty classroom right now buzzes inside her. She jumps onto her bike and takes off, turns left at the railway station. There are some men sitting quietly on a bench and their eyes – some cloudy, some razor sharp – follow her as she whizzes by. Today she's going to do something she's never allowed to do – she's going to ride really far. Farther than she's ever ridden by herself before. The wind whistles through her hair and cardigan, but she doesn't put on a jacket. That would ruin the illusion that it is almost summer. The train rushes by on her left. Its deep, hollow whistle sounds eerie at night, but now she shouts happily in response, racing the train.

After half an hour, she arrives at a field full of cotton-grass, billowing in the gentle breeze. She hops off and leaves her bike by the side of the road. Birgitta walks among the white tufts, running her hands through them. When she reaches the middle of the meadow, she lies down. All she can see is blue sky, interrupted by the occasional cloud or puff of cotton-grass. She closes her eyes, and everything turns red behind her eyelids. She stays like that for a long time. Listens to the next train pass by in the distance. The ground is cold, and it seeps into her clothing, but her stomach and her face remain warm in the sun. After a while she stands up and starts picking flowers. Her bouquet looks like a fat, white rabbit, and she stashes it in her bicycle basket before reluctantly taking off for home again.

At around five o'clock, Valdemar and Margit arrive at the house. Birgitta is reprimanded by her mother. She's not very good at staying on the right side of the road when she rides her bike.

'I get worried,' says Margit.

'I was careful!' Birgitta replies indignantly, then her face softens, and she points to the bouquet on the kitchen table. 'Isn't it nice?' Margit's face softens, too.

It's sausages and leftovers for dinner, pancakes with lingon-berries for dessert. Birgitta eats and eats. There's nothing better than pancakes as far as she's concerned. She stays at the dinner table longer than anyone else. She certainly doesn't have a stomach-ache anymore, her parents say and roll their eyes. When Birgitta's stomach is round and tense like a drum from eating so much, she heads off to Cecilia in the kitchen. The nanny asks her if she wants to dry the dishes, but Birgitta doesn't want to. She heads on towards the parlour. Valdemar glances up from his newspaper.

'Who's clearing the dandelions today?' he asks.

A few seconds of silence follow. Then Birgitta sighs, lifts her shoulders to her ears and lets them drop in resignation again.

'Me.'

It's a pink and shimmering evening, but the heat has fled with the sun, a reminder that it's still just spring. Birgitta pulls up dandelions and throws them into a bucket. When she tires of it, she goes over to swing for a while. Then she helps her mother carry in firewood. They both end up sweaty and rosy-cheeked. When they're done, Margit says:

'Why don't you go to bed now, since you had a stomach-ache today?'

That makes Birgitta mad. She wants to be outside. She feels fine now, like she told them. And all other children are still out. She points to the road where the neighbours' youngest is toddling around.

'Even the babies are out, Mama!'

Margit gives in.

Valdemar is in the parlour, listening to the evening news with Eva in his lap. It's almost seven o'clock. Birgitta enters and walks over to them. Hunches down in front of her little sister, grabs her chubby hand in her own and pushes the icy tip of her nose into Eva's round, warm cheek until she's squealing with laughter. Then she says goodbye and never comes home again.

My first contraction arrives on 19 July. We just got home the night before from two weeks in Corfu. I was only able to eat yoghurt with honey and nuts on that trip, sometimes a little moussaka. I started crying one night in the corner of a restaurant because I couldn't eat, and a waiter comforted me.

Now my stomach turns as hard as a stone. I never had any Braxton Hicks contractions when I was expecting Sam so it takes me a while to realise what's happening. The baby is only as big as an apple. Her heart is so fragile, it might stop beating; she could almost slide out without me noticing.

I start feeling better after week 20. Not good, but not like the living dead anymore. I sit with Justus and Sam, consuming baby-sized portions of dinners I never cook. I don't do the dishes, clean, do laundry or pick up Sam, but I try to be present as much as possible. I'm useless as a parent. I'm ashamed of our messy home, and of the fact that I never show my face at his preschool.

Every night I lie in the bathtub watching bath bomb after bath bomb sink to the bottom then float to the surface with a sizzle. Every one contains a surprise. One transforms the surface of the water into a whole galaxy.

Sometimes I muster all my strength and head to the subway stop, drag my way past the shopping centre and on towards the National Library. I have work to do. My job is usually a joy, but now I squeeze out every word. I get stupid when I'm pregnant, my thoughts sticky as caramel. There's only one subject that can hold my undivided attention: Birgitta. In the cold basement of the library I allow myself to read articles about her case for a few minutes here and there, even though I feel guilty. Every single one of them means time away from my family, another ounce of energy not devoted to my son.

My unborn child has started to make herself felt, like a pike fish rolling around inside me. When I found out Sam was a boy, I had to get used to the idea, but I finally settled into the security of it. How much easier it is to be a boy. Boys can be a little stupid, a little ugly, smell a bit and wear torn clothes without suffering much for it. It was a relief.

Being a girl means facing real danger. When I was lying on the hospital bed this time, my stomach sticky with ultrasound gel, and the midwife pointed to the screen and said, 'Look here, it's a little girl,' my heart lifted then sank at once. I know there are predators hungry for girls. How will I protect her?

Weeks pass. Months, too. I'm still in my bathtub. My stomach rises out of the water like a mighty celestial body above a horizon. I circle my hands around it, trying to sense the contours inside. Is that a knee? A rump, a shoulder? My hands take the bump's measure, and I wonder how big she is right now.

As we begin our arduous journey out of the bathtub, my uterus contracts. I feel it in my lower back, followed by a flash of anxiety. These false labour pains are arriving more frequently. I've been dropping off urine samples periodically at the midwife's office to rule out urinary tract infections, but it's offered me no answers. I dry off and douse myself with oil. Close my eyes and rub it over my stomach, which has softened now. But she doesn't react like she usually does. I rub more insistently. Pushing on the sides of my abdomen. Nothing. When was the last time I felt her? Last night, surely? She's always rowdy in the evening. Her limbs thrash around, bending and pushing out the tense skin like a cat trapped inside a sack.

I walk into the kitchen naked, fill up a large glass with water and down it in one go. I pause, trying to feel her. Nothing. I keep refilling the glass, allowing cascades of ice-cold water to rush past the baby in my stomach, and still no reaction. I decide to call the midwife's emergency number. She answers in a cheery voice. I present my problem while downplaying it. It's surely nothing. 'But you're worried,' she replies. 'Yes, a *little* worried,' I laugh. She thinks I should go in.

'In' means the delivery ward. My heart skips a beat or two. I dress myself like a knight preparing for battle, determination on my face. This is my moment to be brave, to be a mother. I'm not going to call Justus. I won't take a taxi. I'll do this myself. It takes me 15 minutes to walk the 450 metres to the tram. I watch helplessly from a distance as two trams stop and then pull away. I manage to catch the third one, which is almost empty.

The trip to the hospital usually takes 45 minutes by tram and commuter train, but it's double that for me today. I miss another train and have to wait. The walk from the station to the hospital is a long one, and the hospital complex itself gigantic. With its multitude of tiny windows this building is like a spider with thousands of black, shiny eyes. I'm dizzy by the time I arrive, and my nausea is worse. That happens when I don't eat regularly. I buy a ready-made sandwich, which I gulp down so quickly it hurts my throat.

I imagine a maternity ward should be hectic around the clock, but when I arrive it's peaceful. I'm shown to a chair in a hallway. They're speaking in soft, calm voices on the other side of the door. Sometimes a laugh rises like a bird's cry. I sit stock still on the chair. Tears start to stream down my face, and a young, blonde nurse comes over with tissues. 'It's your turn soon,' she tells me. I want to scream at the woman on the other side of the door to quit laughing and go home. Obviously, she's fine.

The midwife who meets me has steel-grey hair, strong, skinny arms and horn-rimmed glasses. I melt into her steady hands. I've never wanted to be a child again more than when I am about to have one. As I lie down on the hospital bed, tears run down my temples onto the beige paper. I pull up my sweater, and the midwife brings over a device to listen to the baby's heartbeat. My anxiety has lessened now; I mostly feel sorry for myself and relieved that this will soon be over. She listens. Moves to another spot and listens again. Pushes on my stomach and changes position again. I try to be helpful.

'I think she's lying in that direction.'

She lifts and listens. Lifts and listens. I try to interpret her face. Here it comes, she takes a deep breath, almost imperceptibly, and holds it for a moment before saying:

'I'm just having a little trouble finding her heartbeat.'

I knew it. Somehow I always knew I wouldn't be allowed to keep her. I start to sink. I fall straight down through the

37

protective paper, through the bed, through the linoleum floor, the wet earth, the gravel, the bedrock, down into the very core of the earth. I descend to Hades to search for her, as Demeter did for Persephone. Just like Demeter, I deny my daughter's death. It's only human to forbid Hades to take the one you love.

Suddenly, I'm pulled out of this blind groping by a familiar, swooshing rhythm, like water rushing through gravel. The midwife says the baby is laying in a way that made it hard to find her heartbeat, but now she sounds just fine. I barely take in what she's saying, but my body understands, allows the insight to register in time with that heartbeat. My beloved. That beloved heart. Never leave me.

My cheeks are burning as I begin my journey home again. I feel ashamed to have worried.

Birgitta goes out to climb on her bike again and discovers it's gone. Karl must have taken it. She walks over to the Blom family's house and knocks on their door. The father opens it, and Birgitta curtsies quickly.

'Can Bittie come with me to the football field? I'm heading there to get my bike.'

He doesn't say a word. Instead, his wife shouts from inside the house that Bittie is about to take her bath. Birgitta curtsies again and heads out to the road. Bittie's father watches her silently before closing the door.

Birgitta is meandering down Gustavsborgsvägen when she catches sight of Miss Petrén in a flowery dress. At school her teacher always wears a dark dress. Just a few days ago, Birgitta was sitting at her desk watching dust float in the stuffy air, and Miss Petrén started telling them about flora and fauna. The teacher took out a stick with a hook at the end and pulled a chart down on the wall. Birgitta was transfixed by an illustration of the pink cones of the larch trees. She'd never seen anything like it before.

'They're in bloom right now, in May and June, and they sprout such beautiful cones,' the teacher had said.

Paradise flowers, Birgitta thought.

Her clogs rattle her legs as she runs to catch up with Miss Petrén, who's walking briskly in the direction of the village. Birgitta is out of breath by the time she swings around on the gravel to greet her teacher with a curtsey.

'Good day to you, Miss Petrén, do you know where those trees grow?' she says.

The teacher stops, places an arm around Birgitta's shoulders and looks down at her sternly.

'I thought you were at home with a stomach-ache today, Birgitta?'

Birgitta turns red and kicks at a stone.

'Yes. But it passed.'

Miss Petrén stares hard at Birgitta as if trying to determine the truth, but reaches no conclusions. She's more interested in her own Friday night plans than in lecturing her students. She does enough of that during work hours.

'You mean the larch?'

Birgitta looks confused for a second then answers. 'Yes, that's right, the larch.'

The teacher smiles.

'Well, you know, there are a few right behind the old football field.'

Birgitta nods again and takes off running down the street again. She turns left at the end, heads past the new football field and down to the old one near the forest. The firs rise up high and dark above the uneven turf. It's a wild wood, easy to get lost in. The children don't often go there alone. Near the entrance, Birgitta sees two boys – the Blom's oldest boy, Åke, and another of Karl's friends. She jogs over to them with an annoyed frown between her eyebrows.

'Where is Karl?' she asks.

He's picking up Åke's ball, she learns. They tell her flippantly, and immediately turn away. A few minutes later, Karl whizzes back on Birgitta's bike with an innocent look on his face. She demands it back, but he begs to keep it just for the evening, so he can play football as long as possible.

'I have to be home by half past seven.'

Birgitta mumbles about needing to be home then, too, then kicks her foot in the gravel and gives in, as little sisters do. She lingers at the entrance, unsure of what to do next. It feels like defeat to head home again. She watches the boys kicking balls. Birgitta often plays with the boys. She's a fast runner and likes tag. But football isn't for girls. She stares up at the tall, black spruces now swaying in the wind. The wind is rising.

A fourth boy arrives. It's Bengt Sommer. He's 14 years old. Karl's good friends with his little brother Axel, even though Bengt's father works at the factory on the Isolite press, making toilet seats. Bengt leans back against the fence a few metres from Birgitta. One of the boys asks if he'd like to join, but Bengt says that he can't, he's headed home to eat soon. Birgitta is restless. She casts a last look at the boys. Then she heads off, walking back towards the new football field.

Shortly after Birgitta leaves, another boy arrives, pulling his little brother behind him in a wagon.

'Åke,' he shouts, 'Sonja wants her bike!'

Sonja is the Blom family's nanny. Like Birgitta, she has discovered that a boy has borrowed her bicycle. Åke looks up and sees the young woman approaching. He runs over and grabs the bike and meets her at the entrance. Åke's cheeks are rosy and his hair stands up on end. Sonja snatches the handlebars angrily.

'Why didn't you bring my bike back?'

She turns away without waiting for an answer and runs after Birgitta, who's walking slowly and somewhat aimlessly down the road.

'Do you want company on your way home?' Sonja says when she catches up. 'I can give you a ride if you want.'

They're nearing the new football field and a clump of laughing and howling boys. Birgitta answers curtly with her eyes on the ground:

'No, I'm staying out longer. Ride on home.'

Sonja knows Birgitta quite well, because Birgitta plays so often with her employer's children. Besides, Sonja is good friends with the Sivanders' nanny, Cecilia, who's also 17.

Birgitta's tone surprises her. She's not usually that curt. Sonja glances sideways at her. Her neck is bent, her mouth pursed. Her body language says she wants to be left alone. Sonja slows and walks the bike just behind Birgitta with her eyebrows raised. A young man in dark golf pants and canvas shoes comes running past them in the direction of the changing rooms at the new football field. It's Bengt. He meets Birgitta's gaze and smiles, and she smiles back.

'Is that why you want to stay out longer? Because of him?' Sonja says it teasingly, maybe to lighten the mood a bit.

'You're so stupid, Sonja,' Birgitta sulks.

As they pass by the entrance to the new football field, a man in a dark suit appears on a bicycle, riding straight towards them. Edvin Oskarsson, Karl's soccer coach.

'Look out!' Sonja shouts to Birgitta, but at that very moment Birgitta crosses the road and starts walking back in the direction they just came from. At the entrance to the new football field, which Edvin Oskarsson and Bengt just entered, Birgitta stops.

There are a few boys throwing javelins and an elderly man raking the tracks around the field. Sonja is uneasy about leaving a girl alone there. She looks for any other women but sees no one. It's not quite seven thirty, and the sun is still up. The Sivander family usually want their children home at half past seven. Birgitta will be leaving soon, Sonja assumes, shrugs her shoulders, climbs on her bike and pedals off towards her relative in the neighbouring village.

Birgitta is left behind. Her face is serious. The wind picks up, and her hair whips into her face. She takes a step towards the darkness of the woods.

The year is 1948. Children and teenagers have no real sense of time. People remember incorrectly. Adults might glance at a station clock on their way somewhere. The maids set their clocks to the radio or the factory whistle, clocks that often run too fast or too slow. Some deliberately set them forward a few minutes, hoping to get up earlier. Then they forget that they did so.

When you average out every indication of the time when Birgitta disappeared, you end up at around seven thirty. That's the time the police settle on. But the witnesses, with few exceptions, had little access to clocks. It's not easy to determine who might have had the time to murder her.

One day I google Birgitta's name and end up on a website about murders in Sweden. Exactly five lines have been posted there about her case. And below it there's a comment:

The information on this page is completely wrong.
I know this BECAUSE I AM BIRGITTA'S *big brother.*
Contact me, and I can tell you.
Best
Karl Sivander

It was written almost four years earlier. In seconds I have his mailing address. Birgitta's older brother. A few days later, I write that address on an envelope. After rewording my letter many times over the course of a couple of weeks, I'm finally ready to send it. I sign it with my name, address, phone number and email.

It doesn't take long for Karl to reply. He does so via email. First he has typed up my letter, then he's created a Word document four pages in length. It's a summary of his family's history, of the murder and of the time immediately after. I email him back and ask if he'd like to meet. If he doesn't want to, I'll abandon all of this, I tell myself. I'm almost hoping he'll say no. But he doesn't.

My arms are wide open for You.
Name a time, and I'll serve you coffee with a slice of toast.
Kind regards
Karl

His arms are wide open for me.

In the case file, there's a note. It's turned brown with age. It was written by someone in blue ink:

Attention! The minor's name should not be shared.

The minor they are referring to is their prime suspect. If you search Birgitta's name in the National Library's archive, you will find it in 125 articles. This boy's name doesn't appear in any of them. The first time I read it in the police files, my stomach sinks. Bengt Sommer. When I search for the name, I find, to my surprise, that Bengt is alive.

It takes even longer for me to write to him than it did to write to Karl. I try to leave things open in my letter. I'm afraid of scaring him off. I'm afraid of other things too.

I receive no reply.

Justus and I travel to Gothenburg at the beginning of October. The train doesn't arrive there until half past ten at night. The hostel we stay in is an old ship, an impressive sight in the autumn darkness. Once inside our tiny room, which is as far below deck as you can go, it's hard to tell you're even on a ship. There's no perceptible rocking. There are no windows. I'm used to going to sleep at nine o'clock, so I fall into bed and sleep deeply and dreamlessly. We eat at the breakfast buffet before going out the next morning, and when we get off the ship, I call Karl.

He answers with a rumble that begins deep in his chest and rises, an ascending scale:

'Heeeellooo, this is Karl.'

I'm surprised that his accent is neither from Skåne nor Gothenburg, but rather Stockholm. He comes to meet us with his little black poodle. He looks much younger than his 82 years. We shake hands and chat on the short walk back to his house, which is located on a hill. I waddle slowly, panting. My stomach is so big now that I'm in the thirtieth week. While I huff and smile, I learn Karl was taught not to talk to journalists. I understand this is because the family were hounded by the press in 1948, and I suddenly feel guilty for being here. Why am I here anyway, and how can I justify it morally? I was taught that there's nothing more important in life than being a good person.

Karl offers us coffee and cake with cream; his wife is away, but she baked before she left. Coffee makes me feel sick these days, so I take a glass of water instead. He leads us into the living room and begins by telling us about Erik, his and Birgitta's little brother. I don't know much about him, but when I didn't find him online I had assumed he was dead. The only image of Erik I found came from a website that sells pictures from the *Svenska Dagbladet* newspaper's archive. They had a portrait of Birgitta there, the one circulated in all the newspapers, as well as two photos from the funeral. For 180 kronor, you could get both.

The first photograph depicts six girls carrying Birgitta's coffin. They wear matching white dresses and white shoes with white socks. Large bows sit by the sides of their serious faces. The second one shows the grieving family. Erik is the little boy on the left, with a confused expression on his face. He's holding a bouquet of lilies of the valley in one hand, his father's hand with the other. His parents and Grandfather Harald are a single unit. They gaze in various directions, their faces express different emotions. The two men stand arm–in–arm with Margit as if she were a tall, beautiful vase with two handles. She's elegant, dressed in deep mourning black, looking to the side. Valdemar and Harald are wearing top hats. Valdemar appears both intensely tired and sad. The photo almost looks like a film still.

Karl stands on the other side of them. He's holding nobody's hand. Both brothers are dressed in white. I bought the pictures and can't explain why. They're lying at home in my desk drawer; I don't know what to do with them. As I sit opposite Karl now, I feel as though I have stolen something from him.

'Erik grew odd,' Karl says.

He was good at school, did well in his written exams, got good grades, but the oral exams tripped him up. One of them went very badly, and so he never graduated. And after that he was odd. In my mind, I can see the boy Erik, trying so hard to make his parents proud, and when it's not enough, he loses his balance and falls. Karl gives me a few fragments of memory:

Erik going to buy new trousers, obsessing over one pair in the clothing store. He latches on to them and sits up all night with his mother talking about the trousers. He goes for some kind of treatment in Lund. He meets a nurse there, and the two fall in love. They have a daughter. The day after his daughter's sixth birthday, he lies down in a bathtub and takes his own life.

Karl goes down into his basement and comes back up with a dusty painting. It depicts Birgitta exactly as she was in the *Svenska Dagbladet*'s archival photo. In a white dress with small puffed sleeves and Peter Pan collar, large bow in her childish bob — a typical style for the time. She has the exact same clothes and hair as the girls who bore her coffin. Is it a coincidence? It looks like a uniform. A collective girls' uniform.

Karl tells us that the painting is quite special because it was actually painted on top of a photo. He's promised it to a museum on Åland that specialises in these kinds of portraits. The museum has some connection to the Rosengren photo studio in Perstorp where that photo of Birgitta was taken. Does he feel sad to part with the portrait? He says no.

'It's not that I want to forget Birgitta,' he reasons. 'That's not why. But right now, it's just collecting dust.'

We take the painting out onto the patio so I can take a picture of it in brighter light. It's grey out and tiny, invisible drops of water hover in the air. Karl holds up the painting.

'Does it look like Birgitta?' I ask. 'Is this how you remember her?'

'Yes,' replies Karl, 'it does.'

I stare at it for a long time. The portrait is, of course, very similar to the photo, because that's what lies beneath the paint, but it feels like something's been added. She looks older in the painting. There's a heaviness and a certainty in her eyes. I've gathered that she wasn't always so deferential. I imagine her as a leader, someone who's not afraid to be loud. Maybe, in some hidden corner of the schoolyard, she teaches the other little girls how to swear. Or maybe I'm being unfair, treating her like an empty vessel that I fill with my own values.

After we start recording the interview itself, Karl has a lot to say. When I ask him what Birgitta was like as a person, he fumbles for the words, and they slip away. I see how the memories become instantly too enormous, a tornado inside him. A shadow passes over his eyes, and his face suddenly turns ageless. I recognise the boy at the funeral.

The evening sun shines between the slender trees when Elin Sjöberg goes out to dig in her vegetable plot. It's the evening of Birgitta's disappearance. As she opens the door, her dog, a St Bernard, starts barking madly at the forest. Elin knits her brow. The dog is usually so good-natured and calm. Now her tail is low and tensed, her eyes so wide the whites are visible. The dog tries to make a run for it, but she's held back by the leash. She throws herself in the direction of the forest with such angry despair that she almost strangles herself. Elin exchanges a confused look with her husband who's now come out too.

'We have to take her inside,' he says.

They manage to get the dog back into the house. Inside, she goes wild. Jumping at the windows, clawing to get out. Elin leaves, but the sound of barking follows her through the garden.

The vegetable plot is approximately twenty-five metres from the house. After about a quarter of an hour Elin has managed to dig through half of it. She stops to breathe and wipe the sweat from her forehead. When she looks up, she notices something unexpected. The last rays of the sun are shining beautifully on the clearing near the river, and a man appears between two birches. He's almost naked – his only clothing is a pair of dark swimming trunks. On his head there might be a dark beret, or perhaps he has dark hair. She watches him for a moment before resuming her work. After she's done, she goes back inside to her husband and dog, who's still barking.

'What kind of fellow was that, sunbathing at this time of day,' she wonders aloud.

Her husband didn't see the stranger. The dog keeps jumping and trying to get out for another hour, until nearly nine o'clock.

Mimmi picks me up at home to drive me to Perstorp. In a few months, she'll become my daughter's godmother. This coming weekend is one reason; our friendship is about to go from good to close. I don't have a licence, and Mimmi is amazing to travel with; an enthusiastic and glamourous companion.

Once, when Sam was little, she took me on an excursion to Kyrkogårds Island, which was once used to isolate people infected with cholera and later became a graveyard for sailors. 'Pack a bathing suit,' she told me. She brought cava and real glasses, a picnic blanket and food. We sat in the sun and drank until our brains turned a little mushy, and then we climbed further up onto the rocky island, to a wild height. Settled down on a rock. Below us lay the dead sailors and cholera victims. We sat in silence with our eyes closed.

Later, in the hostel's outdoor dining area, we heard a woman calling a child's name. She was shouting, her voice getting louder, more desperate. Then she was joined by a man's voice. And then more voices. The woman jogged across the yard, her eyes desperate, searching for her daughter. A huge, meandering fort sits on that island, and you can walk inside it. Its rooms and passageways lie beneath ground level and most don't have ceilings, so it's easy to fall. We joined in the search, scattering in various directions, shouting the name. I was running towards the sun, which shone bright and white, when suddenly the ground ended in front of me. A cliff. My heartbeat felt metallic. I saw it in front of me – a tiny body in a dress, lying in a strange position, completely still.

But when I looked down, she wasn't there. A moment more, and she was found. Later, I saw the family at a picnic table, eating dinner as though nothing had happened. But a part of me couldn't let go of the thought that in some parallel universe she was lying at the bottom of that cliff.

Now it's late autumn, and I'm heavily pregnant, and nervous. Mimmi and I will be away for two nights. What if I go into labour? An uncanny suspicion flashes into my mind: by being here, am I inviting something dark into my womb, exposing my baby to something? That irrational feeling soon passes.

We stay at a historic hotel in Huskvarna for the night. Mimmi tells me about her childhood and points out where she once lived.

Everything takes so much longer than planned the next day. We arrive later than expected in Perstorp, and at first it feels like a relief, as we encounter lovely old houses, lots of green. The soft rain seems life-giving. But we're being deceived. This isn't Perstorp, but the surrounding area, which retains some trace of a romance that has been extinguished in the industrialised centre of town. When we enter Perstorp itself the rain intensifies, falling on abandoned homes with boarded-up windows. A father is dragging his child by the arm. Two women radiating hostility walk across the grocery store parking lot. We drive through the city centre, feeling out of place.

I've compared new and old maps, and I guide Mimmi to the football field. What they call the new football field in the investigation is still here, looking neglected. The old field has been replaced by a parking lot. The rain thunders relentlessly against the car's roof and windows as we pull in.

People seem suspicious. We realise this when car after car slows down on the road. One creeps by us and parks not far away. Nobody climbs out. We start to feel uneasy.

'Should we really . . .?' Mimmi wonders.

Even after driving all this way, we hesitate. Should we even go out in this storm?

'You can stay in here,' I say finally.

I have to get out of this car, even if everything inside me screams not to. I grab my rain poncho and try to pull it on. I'm clumsy. My belly is large and round, my legs wedged beneath the glove compartment. I pull the hood over my head, open the door and waddle out.

It's about a quarter to eight in the evening. Valdemar has just carted away some scrap metal from their yard and run into the forester. The two ended up talking for a long time. Now he's just stepped back into the yard, and Margit comes out to meet him.

'The lawn is full of mole holes,' she says, opening her arms in resignation.

They're discussing what to do about it, when Karl sticks his head out the window of his second-floor bedroom.

'Isn't Birgitta home yet?' he shouts down to them.

Margit shakes her head.

'That's strange,' says Karl, 'I just got home from the football field, and she left before me.'

Margit asks him to take his bike out to look for her. Karl runs downstairs and out the door, grabs the bike and dings his bell happily before continuing out into the street. On the way, he runs into his friend Åke again and asks if he's seen Birgitta. He hasn't. Karl stops. He forgets what he rode out for. It's still light out, and many children are outside. No one's very worried.

Valdemar enters the house and turns on the radio. It's a quiz programme called *Our Conductor*. Valdemar listens to the programme until it ends at eight o'clock. It's time to bike over to the factory for the night shift. The road there goes by the football field. As he passes, he looks for Birgitta, but only sees two men raking. He hears some children, too. They're laughing, or shrieking. It sounds like it's coming from the far side of the changing rooms. He checks the creek to be sure. Then he cycles on.

Valdemar has been at work for a little more than an hour when he hears his wife's voice below his office window.

'Is Birgitta here?'

He rushes down the stairs, unlocks the door and meets her on the gravel. She stumbles over her words while telling him she's been out searching. Shouting. Valdemar thinks of all the random people who work at the factory. Faceless men, who come and go as they please. The two of them bike down to the new football field. But it's dark, and they can't see anything. Valdemar hurries home and one by one he calls all of their friends and acquaintances to ask if Birgitta is with them. She's not. He asks them to bring flashlights and lanterns. Then he calls the Home Guard. The forester and Mr Blom set out, while Valdemar searches the storeroom for parts to assemble a lantern. There aren't enough of them for everyone. Ahead, the forest lays dark and silent.

I'm standing on the new football field. Or the only football field these days, which hasn't been new for a long time now. There's a derelict ticket booth at the entrance. I stare into the forest, then back towards the other direction, at the city centre. That's where most of the workers and their children lived. My gaze wanders to the right where the Sivander house used to stand – the nicer part of Perstorp, where people had servants. And then further to the right, below the forest. That's where Elin Sjöberg's farm once stood, where a half-naked man stepped out into the clearing.

I've just started walking towards the forest when I hear a car door slam shut. Mimmi is jogging towards me. She's dressed in black, wearing high heels and fake fur, and carrying an umbrella. She's not prepared for a walk in a wet forest, but says she can't leave a heavily pregnant woman in the lurch. It's raining so hard now, and everything is slippery and overgrown. The cars driving by have black windows. We step into the trees.

At three o'clock in the morning, the Home Guard forms a human chain and starts to move east from Gustavsborgsvägen. Several hundred men walk side by side, spaced just a few metres apart. Birgitta's name is sung out into the darkness with no particular rhythm. The forest stirs uneasily as the light of the lanterns dances over tree trunks, rocks and moss. Tiny white dots reflect it. Budding lilies of the valley.

One of Valdemar's colleagues, an engineer named Näs, is among the searchers. In the shaky light of the lantern, he sees something up ahead. Is it a circle? As he comes closer, he sees that it's ground that's been trampled.

He yells 'Halt!' and the entire human serpent freezes, beginning with him and rolling in two opposing waves.

Something glimmers on the edge of the circle. He lifts the lantern. A pair of clogs, child-sized. They're standing next to each other, slightly more than half a metre apart. As if someone had a shoe in each hand and calmly, quietly put them down. He walks over and picks one up. There's a crack in the sole. And something dark there. Näs shivers. He starts running out of the forest, down towards the football field.

A group of men are waiting there. He passes them all, until he arrives at Valdemar.

'Is it Birgitta's?' Näs asks, holding out the shoe.

Something deserts Valdemar's face as he stares down at it. Even the youthful hollows beneath his cheekbones seem to sink, dark circles appear around his eyes. He nods.

'Yes, that's Birgitta's.'

Up in the forest, Margit has reached the other shoe. A scream echoes over the spruces.

The forester is standing just outside the trampled circle. While the other men talk quietly among themselves, he looks around. Which way would an animal go? He senses a shape, a movement, over the ground, between branches and thickets. The tracks lead him further up into the woods. There's almost no wind now. Tree trunks rise suddenly in the lantern light and loom over him. The clouds have blown away, and the stars follow the hunter as he walks forward, slow and focused. It takes five minutes, but it might as well have been a thousand years. A pile of stones lies in a watery ditch. The forester feels feverish. There's a ringing in his ears; he is at sea amid a storm. Beside one of the stones, a pale hand rises out of shallow water. He feels his body start to tremble. His voice sounds like someone else's as he calls out for the police.

Do I even know what I'm looking for? I can see the crime scene photos in front of me. A narrow depression. The tracks of a child's sock–clad feet in mud and moss. Where the depression has filled with water, a large stone. A dress beneath. I stumble forward blindly, searching. A sentence from *Agnes Cecilia* runs through my head: *Go I Know Not Whither and Fetch I Know Not What.*

The rain pours down. It feels despicable that Birgitta died in this disgusting place. Heavy, horrible firs. Wet, rotting layers of last year's leaves. Bare branches. I don't know where Mimmi might have gone. And I'm afraid someone else will show up and angrily ask me what I'm doing there. I walk across the road and call out, a bit uncertainly, unsure who might be listening.

'Mimmi?'

No response. Water is running from my hood into my eyes and mouth. I rub my hands over my face, but they too are wet. Then I notice something.

Among the trees that stand between Bruksvägen and Gustavsborgsvägen, the ground sinks into a furrow. And there. What's that? A white circle? I hear a voice say: *Here it is.* It's my voice, but not me saying it. A truck rumbles by on the road I just left. The voice repeats: *Here it is. Here it is. Here it is.* Heavily, I walk forward between brush and branches. As I get closer, I see they're feathers. White feathers. A bird's been killed here. The bird itself is gone. And there, next to the circle, lies the ditch. Here it is. I found her.

Police Constable Ivar Björk and Senior Constable Knut Magnusson follow the sound of shouting. They stumble over stones and swat fir branches out of their faces as they rush forward. When they reach the ditch, they see the forester. His face is lit from below by the lantern in his hand. He points a pale finger downwards. Until this moment, all has been still here. But now the scene is set in motion; beneath the surface, something is moving. The rustling and snapping of twigs is getting closer, and District Police Superintendent Tydén arrives. He has Parish Constable Gottfrid Andersson in tow. Tydén stops, and the parish constable moves closer.

The others form a semicircle around him, while he straddles the ditch and lifts the stone away. A girl's face becomes visible beneath it. The left cheek is twisted to the night sky. Without thinking, he plunges his hands into the icy black water and lifts her head, turning it upwards. Unseeing eyes gaze up at the Milky Way. The parish constable knows it's Birgitta. But Birgitta is no longer there, really. She's sitting atop a tall fir, staring down on these men. Then she takes a deep breath and sets out, rising up towards the arching sky.

We sit in silence on our drive away from Perstorp. The heavy rain has been replaced by dense fog. The baby is sleeping in my stomach. It takes about four hours to get to Borkhult Lapphem, where we've booked a room for the night. The last stretch of our trip is surreal. In pitch darkness, we drive tiny, winding roads through forests and past fields. Mimmi edges forward. In the headlights, we catch glimpses of wild animals. They crawl in the ditches, cross the road like ghosts. Eyes flash and glow. I watch for them so intensely that I have a pounding headache by the time we arrive at half past ten.

The hostel is in old workers' housing from the end of the 19th century. The woman who greets us tells us we're the only guests. She leads us up a narrow staircase, the floorboards creaking underfoot as we enter our room. The wallpaper is a hypnotic jumble of green flowers. Mirrors, wavy with age, hang on the wall. Behind the white lace curtains in the windows there stretches nothing but dark fields and forest. The woman leaves and closes the door behind her.

We don't have anything with us for dinner, and there are no restaurants or shops here, so we snack on some nuts we had in the car. Mimmi observes that the vibe of the place seems a little weird. I go to wash my face. Then — a shrieking. Fear vibrating through my body, I jolt and drop toothpaste onto the floor. It takes a moment for me to realise it's the fire alarm. I walk out and find Mimmi standing on a chair. She's banging at the smoke alarm, but nothing happens. Finally, she tears it down and removes the battery. The silence turns compact. We air out the room, searching for any reason it might have started howling. We find none.

'What happened?' I say.

'I placed the tarot deck there.' The deck is on a small table just below the fire alarm. 'And then it started howling.'

We love ghost stories, but I can see that she's afraid. Usually so easily frightened, now I'm calm. Mimmi points to the rocking chair in the corner.

'It feels like someone is sitting there, a woman. A deeply religious woman. And she doesn't like that I pulled out a tarot deck.'

'You didn't light a candle or anything?'

'No, nothing.'

That night I dream of a stream of people walking through the building. Mimmi has an intense nightmare that also takes place inside the building, a feeling that she is unwanted there. When we awake the next morning, the sky is a light grey. We chat a bit with the owner's mother while eating our breakfast. When we tell her about the fire alarm, she chuckles.

'That's the old lady messing with you,' she says.

At sunrise, Valdemar and Margit head home in mute despair. Constable Björk orders a subordinate to stay at the scene with a search dog while he calls for reinforcements. He hunts down Parish Constable Andersson. The parish constable mentioned one man had been behaving strangely and claimed to be leaving Perstorp that very day. Together they head over to the barracks at the acetum factory where the man's been staying. They arrest him on the spot and search his room, but find nothing and allow the man to go free. Later, all of the papers with his name on them are thrown away.

By a quarter to seven the sun is high, and the birds are shrieking. Senior Constable Magnusson and Constable Björk slam their car doors down by the football field. They head to the spot where the clogs were found. The right shoe has a crack in the toe, shaped like a T. There's blood visible, and a strand of hair caught in the crack. There is a circle of trampled and kicked-up moss of about half a metre in diameter. Just to the west of it, there's a smattering of blood on the leaves, like tiny dark rubies.

They walk over to the ditch and stare down. The prints of feet in socks are clearly visible in the mud. Larger, shod footprints follow behind. Balance is lost and a half step taken backwards. He's still after her. Birgitta seems to have been attacked initially where the clogs were found, managed to run 60 metres then jumped into the ditch, where she changed direction and took nine steps before being attacked again and beaten to death. Constable Björk pours plaster into one of the shoe prints.

Where the footprints end there's a pile of stones and an uprooted stump. Birgitta's body still lies beneath them. The killer seems to have tried to hide her. A clumsy attempt. A light outline is visible in the dark water, but she is almost completely submerged. The rock that the parish constable lifted from her face now lies beneath her chin. It's smooth, about fifteen by twenty centimetres in size. The largest stone sits atop her chest and stomach. In order to reach it, four smaller stones had to be removed first. You can see the hollows on the side of the ditch where they sat biding their time for centuries. Now they've fulfilled their destiny. Like flowers thrown into an open grave, soft and light.

When the stones are lifted away, Birgitta's body is exposed. She's lying on her back with her feet close together. Her right arm is bent at a right angle, palm up, fist loosely clenched. The other hand is pressed to her chest.

The girl is bare-headed, clad in a blue wool cardigan, slightly wrinkled but not dishevelled, a multicoloured tiny checked dress, wrinkled on the left side, panties, socks, of which the left one is rolled down to the ankle.

Beneath the surface of the water, at the place where her head rests, they find a pyramid-shaped stone with its tip pointing up. It sits deep. A grown man can stand on its tip without it sinking. The police dig up the stone and take it with them. They search for a murder weapon, but don't find one.

Justus and I are sitting on the sofa, I'm propped up on every pillow in our apartment. Like a sultan, enthroned with my big belly. Sam is with my parents. My contractions have started three times, then subsided after a few hours. We're watching the last *Harry Potter* movie. I have a nearly empty box of chocolates in my lap. Only the yucky ones are uneaten. In my left hand I'm holding a small control, which is connected by wires to electrodes on my back. It's a TENS machine that's supposed to provide pain relief during labour. Sam's birth took a long time, and I'm prepared to be in pain for a while with this one, too. What I hadn't counted on this time, however, was that the labour pains would come and go for days. Storm then calm, alternating. I gather my strength before every contraction. The electric hum on my lower back is almost pleasurable.

I ask Justus to rewind the film. I've lost track of what's going on. The contractions are arriving more often and getting more intense. I close my eyes and breathe, deep and slow. I'm a primeval animal wallowing in warm mud. My body heaves up and down. Justus says it might be time for a bath. Earlier the labour pains subsided when I did that, a sign that it wasn't time yet. A bath will mean putting down the control and taking off the electrodes. But he's right. He helps me off the sofa. Draws a bath. I sink down. The water is warm. Justus goes out to the living room again. It doesn't take long before I call out to him. The contractions aren't subsiding. They're getting stronger.

An icy full moon is shining outside, but inside the delivery room is awash in the warm light of Advent candles. I've given up on the playlist I prepared, I can't take anything energetic. Instead, I've asked Justus to put on Shida Shahabi's *Homes,* which is something I listen to while writing. I know every single press of the piano keys in it. I plunge into that music and wander across the massif I find there, step by step. Every contraction flows towards a river of snow-melt rushing from the peak. I know I'll never reach the top, I'll die on the way. But I forget that.

Wrapped in those incandescent sounds at the beginning of a song called 'Vassen', I reach the cairn, and she takes her first breath while still inside my body. The midwife says I need to stop pushing. I howl. I am the entire universe, I am pressing up against the force that compels celestial bodies into motion. Everything stops. A billion years go by. Two. Three. Then I fall from the peak, into the abyss. I plunge into the sea as I receive her. It's precisely six o'clock in the morning.

I watch Justus cut the umbilical cord. His eyes are almost spilling over with tears. He sobs as the midwife places Vivi on my chest, and I do the same at the sight of him. Only now am I sure that he wants her. She's wet and warm, her hair slicked back against her head. I pull the hospital's yellow blanket over us. She immediately starts searching for my breast. When she finds it, she calms down. I see she has a V at the top of her forehead. A clear V for Vivianne. 'My love,' I say over and over, crying and laughing. I'm high on hormones and don't even notice the blood rushing out of me. I merely note how they are calmly replacing the pads at regular intervals. The midwife asks if I feel any cramping. No, I'm done right? They massage my stomach. A gruff woman comes in and inserts acupuncture needles. It takes a while for me to realise something's not right. Finally, I see it on Justus's face. Another woman enters.

'Do you feel this?' she wonders.

I feel absolutely nothing. I smile and shake my head.

'Aren't there any longer gloves?' the woman asks someone. She sounds a little agitated.

'I guess I'll have to make do with these.'

She pushes a hand inside me. They keep asking if it hurts, if I feel anything. No. The epidural seems to still be working. But it feels strange when her hand reaches my womb, where my baby was just recently protected from the outside world. Everyone is kind and calm, but it still feels like an assault. An intrusion. She's tearing down a shrine in there. She digs with her hand, loosens the edges of the placenta and gets it out with a sigh. The blood runs over the edges of the blue gloves.

I am not allowed to stand up. They empty my bladder using a catheter. Later they ask me if I think I'm able to get up and go pee. I have no idea, but I'm eager to please and want to seem capable and strong. I stagger into the bathroom. The fluorescent tubes glare. I catch a glimpse of my own ravaged face in the mirror on my way to the toilet. I sit down and hear gentle voices on the other side of the door, coming from the manger where little baby Jesus now sleeps. Then something in my head tilts and flips in my stomach. I'm afraid of sounding weak and wimpy when I say:

'I don't feel so well.'

They enter the moment my body tips to the side. They hold me up and hand me a bag and I vomit and vomit.

When we leave the maternity ward, I'm not holding Vivi. I'm too unstable. I grip the railings that run along the walls of every corridor of the hospital. My dad is picking us up. He has Sam with him. Sam said he wants to go home to Grandma and Grandpa's again afterwards. Now he's sitting on a chair holding his little sister. We help him. His long fringe falls across his face as he bends over her.

'She's so little,' he whispers.

'I know,' I answer.

He lifts her fingers one by one and laughs.

'Tiny, tiny fingers.'

He examines her feet.

'Tiny, tiny toes.'

He waves her feet with his hand then whispers:

'I want to go home with you.'

Senior Constable Magnusson and Parish Constable Andersson make their way resolutely towards the factory barracks. They're both wearing trench coats and hats. The weather is good, and even at this early hour some of the workers and their families have already abandoned the cramped darkness of their quarters. They watch curiously as the two men head in their direction, waiting to find out their purpose.

Many of the workers in Perstorp had fled the war. Most are Sudeten Germans, Poles and Hungarians. One man takes the initiative to greet the senior constable and the parish constable. He speaks Swedish and often acts as interpreter.

'We need all of the men's shoes,' Magnusson replies brusquely, his bushy, fair eyebrows drawn low and stern.

The worker receives no further explanation. He flings his arms wide in a hopeless gesture and heads back toward the small crowd gathered behind him. Soon, knuckles knock loudly on every door of the barracks and worn shoes are lined up in long rows on the grass. The senior constable walks down the row, lifting up each left shoe, examining the underside and then putting it back down again. Those watching mutter to each other. It is a long time before they're free to go. They receive no explanation until they get to the factory. There, among thundering machines, it is whispered that the engineer Sivander's young daughter was found dead. There were footprints in the ditch beside her body. Resentment and outrage rush through their blood. Of course, the police suspected them first.

Vivi. She's born with a funny hairstyle. Dark and straight; thick on the back of her head with a tiny fringe high on her forehead. You can see exactly where she rubbed her skull against my pelvic bone until I screamed in pain. She has a cowlick that makes the hair on top of her head stand straight up and to the side. A little troll nose and a moody mouth. She looks like Justus.

We arrive home earlier than planned, and I wrap her in a soft grey cardigan. I wore it almost every day for months to make it smell like me in the hope that it would give her security. Relatives are visiting and they take turns holding her. I've dressed her in yellow pyjamas, they're Sam's hand-me-downs and way too big for her. She's so tiny. Much smaller than he was when he was born. As soon as our relatives leave, I undress her. It feels unnatural to have her in clothes – she seems more animal than human. I carry her against my skin; she hiccups and yawns, breastfeeds and falls asleep with her nose pressed to my chest. After Sam and Justus leave for preschool it's just the two of us, and I revel in it. Time stands still as I run my eyes over all her rolls and curves. Stroke her hair and her soft little arms and neck. She's like a tiny, naked bulldog. The scent from her head, when you inhale it, is a faint mix of musk and creamy sandalwood.

On the third day we go outside, and I sit on the bench in front of our building. My friend Lovisa comes striding up the hill with a pushchair. Her daughter Lena was born a month before Vivi, and Lovisa already has her routines. She takes very long walks, more than one, every day.

'Yesterday I walked ten kilometres,' she tells me.

I'm frail and weak. On the sixth day, Justus and I walk a short distance to go out for lunch. Everyone who passes by our table seems to stop, their eyes turning warm and kind. Everything in my body hurts, and I have almost no energy. I walk like a dying man. In front of the timber yard I have to stop in the January sun and unbutton to breastfeed Vivi.

One day I'm at our living-room window, which looks out onto a tree with a large magpie's nest in it. Year after year, the magpies return and fix up their nest. We joke about them like they're our neighbours: look, they're renovating again, or they're adding an extension. Justus is in the bathroom changing Vivi, and I'm standing alone in the cold light, watching a single magpie. Then another kind of bird arrives. A pigeon? It behaves strangely. It seems to want to get into the magpie's nest. I'm rocking back and forth as though deranged, as you do when you're used to holding a baby in your arms. Watching, confused, I call out to Justus: 'Come in here, there's some kind of drama outside.' Then it dawns on me: that's no pigeon. That's a hawk. It's hunting the magpie. With rising horror, we watch as our neighbour the magpie almost escapes, but is ultimately overpowered. The hawk pulls it to the ground and starts to eat. The magpie's mate circles above, croaking in despair.

It is 11 days after the birth. We go with my mum and dad to Tyresta National Park. Sam is with us. I feel guilty about him; he hasn't had his mother for so long, and now that the baby is finally here, I just want to be alone with her. I'm having frequent feelings of panic, but I struggle against them. So I go to Tyresta and breastfeed in a shed. On my next visit to the midwife, I tell her about my racing heart, ask if I can keep taking promethazine as a sedative. But it's not allowed when you're breastfeeding. There's nothing to take.

'Go back to the start again,' my midwife tells me. 'Back into the baby bubble. Don't go anywhere.'

I do as she says. We close ourselves off behind blankets and drawn curtains. I only venture out within walking distance, and never go to the store. It works. I grow calm. My heart stops racing.

A shadow moves through Perstorp that May evening. How does a person who's just killed someone feel? Anxious about getting caught, perhaps, though this person need not fear. No one will ever be convicted of the killing of Birgitta, not by the law anyway. Does the killer condemn himself? Or does exhilaration rush through his body, joy, as he passes the warmly lit windows that evening, sees people inside listening to the radio, fixing themselves an evening snack, putting their children to bed? Would Birgitta's killer recognise himself in the description the notorious British 11-year-old murderer Mary Bell gave 20 years later? The adult Mary Bell said to a journalist that she didn't feel angry, she felt nothing. An emptiness and an abyss.

I imagine two alternatives for what the killer might have felt. In the first, anguish arrives like a tidal wave after this grotesque action. In the second, his body was permeated with agony before the murder, but now it's gone, replaced by a silent void.

I hope option one is closer to the truth, because then it may all be over now. If it was the second, then something more will happen.

Bengt Sommer is awoken by voices. Papa's is muffled. Mama's is shrill, and he shudders as it rises to a falsetto. Bengt sits up and looks over at his little brother, who is sleeping head-to-toe with him. Axel's cheeks are still rosy from sleep, and he's blinking drowsily. Bengt pokes him further awake. Together they stare at the closed door and listen intensely. When Bengt hears feet moving across the floor, he calls out.

'Mama? Papa?'

It's quiet on the other side of the wall. Then the door opens. Mama Rut comes in and sits on the edge of the bed, while Papa Otto remains standing, leaning against the door-frame.

'What's the matter?' Axel asks, rubbing his eyes.

Mama's eyes are shiny. She has her head tilted. A sob escapes her, before she puts one hand on Axel's cheek and the other on Bengt's. They're rough and dry.

'Papa just told me something terrible. Mr Sivander's little girl was found dead in the forest. Murdered.'

Axel gasps. He's a good friend of Karl Sivander. Bengt looks at his father, who nods.

'They found her above the football field.' Papa pauses for a moment before continuing. 'You were there yesterday, Bengt. If you saw or heard anything strange, you have to report it. That's very important.'

'No, I . . .' Bengt shoves his hands in his armpits, looks at the window and then back at his father again. 'I just kicked a ball, then I went home.'

Mama stands up, goes over next to Papa, smiling weakly.

'I'm going downstairs to make some hot cocoa. It must be a terrible shock for you.'

It's Saturday afternoon and time for football practice, but it doesn't seem like that's going to happen. Coach and factory worker Edvin Oskarsson is watching the boys on the team. They stand around in small clusters, whispering. A colleague from the acetum factory told him what had happened as soon as Edvin and his landlord Börje arrived for their early shift this morning. By now everyone has heard the news about Sivander's little girl. Edvin is talking to one of the other coaches, but he has his eyes fixed on the boys.

'Do you think a 14-year-old could have done it?' he asks quietly.

The man looks at him with surprise and scepticism in his eyes.

'Why are you asking?'

Edvin looks at Bengt, who's laughing at something another boy just said. Edvin hesitates for a moment before walking over to him.

'Did you see anyone after I met you yesterday? You came from that direction.'

The boys standing closest look at Bengt curiously.

'No, no one.'

'Did you go home after we saw each other?'

'Yes.'

Edvin keeps his eyes focused on Bengt, who's kicking at the gravel. Then he says in a voice loud enough for the whole team to hear him:

'Shall we go up and see where they found the girl?'

Almost all the boys join him. They want to see. A few remain, their eyes on the ground. One of them is Bengt. When Edvin comes back from the woods again, a line of boys trailing behind him, he goes over to him again.

'Have you been up there, Bengt?'
'No.'

After Edvin comes home that evening, Börje wants to discuss what happened.

'You were at the football field yesterday. Did you see something?'

Edvin takes a deep breath and holds it. Then he says:

'There's a boy on the team who's acting a little odd.'

Silence, then Börje answers.

'If someone's acting suspiciously, you have to tell the police,' he says.

Edvin looks out the window, draws his shoulders up in a shrug, holds them there for a moment, then drops them with a long sigh.

'Yeah, I know. I will. But I don't see how that boy could have done it. Maybe it will sort itself out before I even have time to tell the police.'

But Edvin doesn't wait long. By ten o'clock the next morning, he shows up at the police station to tell them that on Friday evening he saw Bengt Sommer walk into the forest.

When I'm alone with both children, stress makes my heart feels like it's going to jump out of my chest. There's only enough of me for one. Sam wants only Justus and pushes me away. I tell him softly that I'll do bedtime, if he wants. I smile, sure that the first time I offer, he'll want me back.

'Noooo,' he says in a sinking whine as he stares imploringly at Justus. 'Daddy . . .'

His eyes fill with tears. He wants his dad to do bedtime. Even though Dad just sits on a chair below his bunk bed, won't crawl up and lie close like Sam wants. Like I would. I try not to show how hurt I feel. Next time I ask, I'll prepare for a no. I can see he senses my insecurity.

When I'm with Vivi, I'm high on endorphins. I love being alone with her. I can't understand why I found it difficult to be alone with my first child, and feel guilty to be so happy now. I'm in love, infatuated. I want to be only, only, only with her. It's not even hard to get up late at night. I'm not that worried. I check periodically to make sure she's breathing, but the fear passes quickly, and without any great anxiety. When Sam was little, I thought my dad's driving would kill us, and was suspicious of everyone on public transport.

In February we celebrate Justus's birthday and Vivi's birth at my mother-in-law's. It's us, my mother-in-law, father-in-law, my mum, dad, sister, Maya and Justus's cousin. Vivi wears a pair of leopard-print pants and a matching onesie. My mother-in-law has baked a chocolate cake, and we drink coffee from tiny cups. We have no idea this will be the last time we meet for a very long time, indoors and carefree. In mid-February, Lovisa and I go to a pushchair-friendly cinema with Lena and Vivi. The movie is *Little Women*. Lovisa and I have been looking forward to being on parental leave at the same time. Our daughters are going to be best friends, I believe. But in fact, they will barely meet each other.

The coronavirus reaches Stockholm. People start squirrelling away supplies. Me too, secretly. I don't want *my* family to go without food. I buy things we never eat. Baked beans in tomato sauce. Canned fish. I stash the food at the back of the pantry.

On Saturday we're planning to attend a 1-year old's birthday party. I feel uneasy. I tell Justus that, and he says we don't have to go if I don't want to. I'm so tired of being the one who worries.

We go to the party early, thinking it won't be crowded yet. It's packed. Everyone's hugging. Friends I haven't seen for years are there. I forget which coffee cup is mine and accidentally take someone else's. It's the last time things are normal.

Bengt is standing at Perstorp's station with his teammates. They're headed off to play a match in Tyringe. One of his friends is holding a newspaper. It's all about the murder of Birgitta.

'Can I take a look?' Bengt says and holds out a hand.

The boy hands it over. Bengt reads the bit about large stones being placed on top of Birgitta's body.

'He must have been one strong bastard,' he says, handing back the newspaper.

A rustle and a murmur make their way through the crowd of boys. They all turn to face the same direction. Bengt, too. Two policemen are headed their way.

'Which one of you is Bengt?' asks one.

His teammates look at him.

'Him,' they murmur.

Both men's eyes are steely when they say:

'You need to come down to the station with us, Bengt.'

It is half past twelve in the morning when constables Magnusson and Björk sit down opposite Bengt. The boy across from them is scrawny, with gaps between his teeth and unruly blonde hair. He looks younger than his 14 years. Narrow shoulders pull up towards his ears while he simultaneously sinks further down into the hard chair. His uncertain eyes reluctantly meet theirs. They ask him to account for his activities on Friday evening. Bengt tells them he went down to the football field when the evening news started at seven o'clock. He lives close by, about

81

a ten-minute walk. He saw some of the boys' team and a group of young men from the office team, who'd just finished playing on the old football field. They were changing their clothes. Then he went with two brothers he knows over to the new football field and kicked a ball around with them. After a while he went back to the old football field again. He met Karl and his friends there. Birgitta was there. Bengt believes he must have been standing about five metres from her. It's hard to say.

'Did you talk to her?'

'No.'

After saying goodbye, he headed over to the new football field again. A young woman he recognised met him coming from the opposite direction. She was walking a bicycle and Birgitta was beside her. He glanced at them. After that his coach, Edvin Oskarsson, passed by on his bike. Bengt called his name, and he stopped.

'When is the other boys' team playing on Sunday?'

'Half past nine.'

Bengt tells them that he followed Oskarsson into the changing room where he saw three men whose names he didn't know. He drank some water and then went out again, headed home.

'When did you get home?'

'Ten or a quarter past eight.'

'How do you know that?'

'I looked at the clock when I got home.'

Both constables narrow their eyes at the boy.

'Are you telling the truth now, Bengt? Did you go straight home?'

Bengt swallows hard.

'Yes, I went home.'

We've lived in the same place, in the same building, for six years, and we need a bigger apartment. I've never liked our current one. It's dark, and I feel the weight of all the people living above us like an iron blanket. Heavy, plodding and angry – we walk around the flat scolding each other. Every day I wander around the neighbourhood feeling crowded by all the people working from home because of the pandemic. I dream of the forest and peace. When we hear of a viewing for a flat in Kärrtorp, bright with high ceilings and a view over the Nacka nature reserve, we are eager to see it.

The open house is well attended. I start smiling as soon as I step inside, because of the view from the kitchen window. Tentatively, I sit on the sofa in the living room and stare outside. From here all you can see are the tops of the trees in the nature reserve. It feels like somebody took a high-rise building and plopped it down in the countryside. With Vivi asleep in her carrier, I climb up the stairs and walk through a door into a small study at the back. It leads out to a balcony. It's a grey March day, and the wind whips around me. It's like climbing to the top of a mountain. When I come back inside, I hear people saying things to each other like 'This is where my room would be,' and 'This is where the kids would sleep.' They feel like intruders; it almost makes me angry. As I go back down the stairs, my eyes meet Justus's. He nods, and I nod back.

It's Sunday, two days after the murder, and the welder Roland Nilsson is walking towards the city park. Perstorp is tense. The flags are flying at half-mast, and mothers hold on to their children with bone-white knuckles. As Roland approaches the park, he sees the lady next door, Rut Sommer. He starts heading over to greet her, but Rut's shoulders are shaking, and her face is buried in her hands. Roland stops. In his head, he adds two and two together. On Friday evening he'd stood outside his house waiting for the bread truck with a watch in his hand. He didn't want to miss the radio play *Kolar-Fredrik*, which was starting at eight thirty. Shortly before eight o'clock, Bengt walked by. The Sommer family's house is about a hundred metres from Roland's. They nodded to each other.

'Did you have a match?' Roland asked, while counting the bread coupons in his hand.

'No, just practice, on the old football field,' Bengt had answered.

Then Bengt asked Roland, who worked part-time at the movie theatre, if he could see a movie that wasn't considered appropriate for children. Roland said that, unfortunately, he couldn't let Bengt go.

On Saturday morning, Roland heard about the terrible thing that had happened. Later in the day, he spoke to the parish constable about the matter. The constable's daughter and her fiancé were there, too. One of them mentioned in passing that football practice had ended at seven o'clock that evening. Roland tilted his head thoughtfully. Why was the boy out so late?

'Someone should really talk to the Sommers' kid. He must have been down by the football field at around the same time Birgitta disappeared.'

The fiancé had looked at him curiously.

'How do you know that?'

'He came home while I was waiting for the bread truck.'

'How did he seem?'

Roland paused, staring off into the distance. He hadn't thought the boy seemed different in any particular way.

'Pretty normal, I'd say.'

The parish constable snorted and glanced away, the daughter narrowed her blue eyes and the fiancé's eyes narrowed even more, if possible. Then he too looked away, toward the edge of the forest, lit a cigarette and said:

'You'll see, somebody young did this.'

'Why do you say that?'

'Just a feeling.'

The daughter looked at him like a wild rabbit.

'Yuck! If it is the Sommers' boy, he has to be mentally disturbed. You can't act normal after something like that. Especially such a young boy!'

Now Rut is standing in the park crying, with the bicycle thrown down next to her. Roland wipes his hands on his pant legs as he walks over to her. Rut has always been a sensitive soul, and he has a soft spot for her. He places a warm, calloused hand on her shoulder, and she flinches, but then leans into him. He holds her awkwardly.

'They've taken Bengt.'

It comes out in spurts. Rut's husband, Otto, just got home and told her their youngest son, Axel, had said that Bengt wasn't at the football match, but down at the police station, under arrest for the murder of Mr Sivander's little girl. Her voice rises into a falsetto.

'And then I said, "My Bengt? Is he up there? Is he at the police station?" And Otto said, "Take it easy, Rut." "Bengt!" I shouted, and grabbed the bike from Otto to ride over there, because I didn't think it was t . . .'

She can't even get the last word out. Rut's whole body trembles, while she sinks to the ground. Roland follows her down and holds her upright while she weeps.

After Rut Sommer gets home and collects herself, there's a knock on the door. It's Senior Constable Magnusson and Parish Constable Andersson. They ask Rut and Otto to tell them about Friday night. Rut's eyes are wild.

'Bengt wanted to go to the football field, but I said he had to try on his suit first. Siv, my daughter, is getting married just after Pentecost. There's so much to do before that, and I told him he had to try it on now, so I'd have time to alter it over the weekend. As soon as we were done, he ran off. He got home just after eight o'clock. I saw that he wasn't wearing the white canvas shoes that his coach gave him, even though he knows I want him to use those when he goes for a kick-about. And now his shoes were dirty. I saw them, and he said, "Yes, they're dirty, Mum." "You go clean them yourself," I said. Take the brush from the cabinet. And I didn't think any more about it.'

She speaks defensively, almost rebelliously. Otto puts an apologetic hand on her shoulder.

'And, how did he seem when he got home?'

Senior Constable Magnusson is the one asking.

'He didn't seem in any particular way,' sniffs Rut, 'he was calm, just like usual!'

Tears well up in her eyes when the senior constable asks to see the shoes and clothes Bengt was wearing Friday, and she gets them. Magnusson turns away from Bengt's parents while he inspects the jacket. His heartbeat quickens when he sees small, dark spots. He lifts up the shoes, a pair of grey athletic shoes from Tretorn, turns them over and inspects the sole.

'I'd like to take the clothes and shoes back to the station, Mrs Sommer,' he says and nods to the parish constable, who takes out two brown paper bags.

In awkward silence, Rut and Otto watch while the senior constable and the parish constable rustle open the bags and place the clothes and shoes inside.

I'm sitting on the balcony of our new apartment, watching swallows play. The view is breathtaking but I'm constantly afraid someone will fall and die. I will be standing on the balcony with Vivi held firmly in my arms, humming and singing and pointing out buildings and trees, and then suddenly a mental image of her little body falling helplessly bursts into my mind. I take a quick step back, as far from the railing as possible. Sometimes I start to fear the balcony collapsing. I can almost feel it happening, feel us falling the 11 floors.

In the mornings, Justus always gets up first with the kids. I'm supposed to sleep in because I'm up breastfeeding at night, but instead I lie awake listening for panicked screams and howls of grief. I imagine one of them falling out of a window or Justus dropping Vivi from the opening between the upstairs and down.

Now the kids are sleeping and I'm sitting in a black-and-white-striped armchair. I sit here every night after the kids go to bed, reading the case files on Birgitta's murder again and again.

I often call or text Karl. The last time we spoke, I asked him if he remembered any of Birgitta's female friends. At the time he didn't, but now I've received an email from him containing a name. I look it up on Facebook and find her immediately. The profile picture shows an older woman with short, light grey hair and glasses low on the bridge of her nose. I do a background check online and conclude she can't be a classmate of Birgitta's; she was born the year Birgitta died.

But through this woman's profile page, I do find a Perstorp Facebook group. I read post after post. One person asks the question:

'Pär Siegård supposedly painted a fresco at the elementary school in 1949. It was donated by the Sivander family in memory of their daughter. Where is it?'

It still stands in Central school's old auditorium. Karl has the original above his piano, and it was displayed proudly when I was there. *Nature. In memory of a girl* is the title. He inherited it from his mother. Someone posts a picture of the fresco. I stare at it for a long time. It covers an entire wall up to the ceiling and depicts wild animals gathered in greenery. I see deer, hares and, on the far right, two large birds. A large sun shines in the centre of the painting. Giant lilies of the valley grow among the animals.

It's 11 August, and I'm changing my daughter's nappy. It's hot, and I allow her to stay completely naked for a while. 'Naked and free,' I sing to her and drag out on the *eee*. She babbles her reply: *Da-da-da*. Smiling at something only she can see on the ceiling above. Then suddenly she's sad. I lift her up. I'm not wearing any clothes either, and I can tell she likes the feel of her skin against mine. She calms down and lays her cheek against my shoulder.

An old mirror with a gold frame is hanging just above her changing table, and I stand in front of it, moved by the sight of her tiny body. It's been seven months and a day since I pushed her out into this world. She's small for her age, but starting to develop that plumpness babies get around now. Her belly is round. Her shoulders slender and sloping, her arms weak and smooth. Her feet rest securely against my stomach, toes angled in towards each other. We look like a painting. Mother and child. An icon. The only sound is the wind blowing through the open windows of our apartment, and my unconditional love streams into her like a rushing, all-consuming river. I run my hand over the folds on her back. I want us to stay together like this forever.

Having her has been the source of my greatest joy and my deepest terror. I tickle her neck with my nose and laugh when she laughs, and the very next moment I'm overcome by dread at what she might experience. How can I prepare her for this life?

Sometimes I think about two sisters I played with one summer, when I was a child. One was 7 and the other 5 and they had a summer house near my grandfather's home. Both were tow-headed and tanned. I slept over at their house once, and the little sister took off all her clothes before we went to bed.

The big sister became embarrassed when the little one said, 'Mum says it's good to sleep naked so you air it out at night!'

That was new to me. I'd never heard anything about my . . . well, what? I remember when the Swedish newspaper *Aftonbladet* had a vote to decide what we should call 'it'. The word that won was '*snippa*'. But to me it felt foreign to call it anything at all. Once, when I was little and swimming in a lake, I slipped and hit a sharp rock. The pain shot up like a red-hot spear between my legs and blood started to flow. But I couldn't tell anyone what had happened when I got home. I didn't know the words. I'd hurt a place on my body that I had no name for, but that I somehow knew was embarrassing.

Now, three decades later, this discussion seems almost stale. Everyone else has moved on. But the words still feel strange in my mouth. Everyone else has left the room before I even had a chance to speak. They've other things to talk about now, in other rooms. The matter has been resolved. Hopefully that will remain the case for Vivi and her generation. But I'm still there. Surely I'm not alone?

Karl fumbles for the words to explain the relationship children had to their bodies in 1948. I think he's trying to tell me someone could have approached Birgitta up in those woods without her making a sound. If there was an assault on her body, on this unknown territory, how would she react? At the time of the murder, the press and the judicial system wondered why no witnesses heard any screams or cries for help. Of course, these days, becoming paralysed in the face of aggression is not considered unusual; it's a defence mechanism, a strategy for survival inherited from our animal ancestors. If a predator attacks, we freeze, whether we have words for it or not. And Birgitta lived at a time when children were expected to be obedient, to offer no objections.

I read the interrogation of the Blom family's nanny, Sonja. She's asked by the court if Birgitta was 'romantic'. Sonja answered yes, that she always talked to boys and looked at them. She also told them that the Sivanders' nanny, Cecilia, called Birgitta 'dreamy'. What was meant by that? That a girl of 9 might behave in a way that encouraged advances? That she might even be promiscuous? Perhaps I shouldn't be surprised that in 1948 people didn't shy away from blaming the victim. But still, I am. I read the interrogation with as much generosity as I can muster, but I arrive at the same conclusion: the judicial system asked if Birgitta behaved in a way that made her a likely victim of sexual abuse.

When Professor Einar Sjöwall enters the room, the girl is already laid out for autopsy. Her body is covered with mud and withered leaves. Cold and motionless. Five more men step into the room, shivering when the cold hits them. The chief doctor at the infirmary, the county police superintendent, the district police superintendent, the senior constable and the hospital's janitor. Do all of them need to be there? Why the janitor? One of the policemen hands over an envelope. Birch leaves with small, dark drops of blood are lying inside. Einar closes it again and begins his examination of the clogs on a separate metal table. They, like the girl, are covered with mud and brown leaves. The mud is carefully scraped away. A strand of hair is stuck in a crack on the right shoe. Einar plucks it out and measures it, examines it under the bright light of the lamp. The strand is 12 centimetres long, thin and blonde. Blood has dripped into the shoe and down to its toe. In heavy silence, Birgitta's garments are laid out one by one on a separate table. There's no blood on the cardigan. Not even the collar. There's no blood on the dress either. Bodice, short underpants and knee socks. All those small, bright clothes are free of blood.

I don't want to describe the autopsy. It's enough to relate what it revealed about the events as they unfolded. This is particularly important, because I know over the years many have wondered if it might have been an accident. Before I read the autopsy report, I asked myself the same thing. But this was no accident.

Birgitta probably received the first blow on her cheek at the site where the clogs were found. That's where the blood-stained leaves were found. Why did she take off her shoes? Or did someone else take them off? I envision her placing the shoes on either side of her feet. Why? From there, Birgitta began to run through the forest in her socks. She managed to get about sixty metres away before jumping into the ditch. The perpetrator caught up with her there and hit her repeatedly on the back of the head, probably with a rock, which was never found. At some point she turned, or more likely was turned, onto her back. There was a small wound on the left side of the jaw. Beneath that the bone was broken. A pyramid-shaped stone was found beneath her head, which matched one of the injuries at the base of her skull.

After reading the autopsy report, I need to pause. I'm sitting at home on the sofa. The apartment is quiet and still, except for the sound of Sam's audiobook playing in his room. Golden light streams from small lamps. The whole scenario plays in my head, rewinds, plays again. I try to understand. Birgitta is in the clearing. Someone with size 42 shoes is coming. Is it someone she knows? The small, round space is tramped down. She takes off her clogs, or he takes them off. They're placed neatly about sixty centimetres apart. Is he the one rolling down her sock? She receives a blow and starts to bleed. But it's not so powerful that she can't run straight. She escapes up into the woods, southwards, jumps into the ditch and changes direction. She runs north. Nine steps. Then a blow to the back of the head. She falls and receives several more at the same place. Presumably he was the one who turned her over, because, according to Einar Sjöwall, she died quickly. She receives blows to the face. No blood is found on her clothes. How is that possible? After Birgitta dies, the perpetrator digs stones and a stump out of the sides of the ditch. It must have taken some time, and whoever did it would have gotten their clothes dirty. He places them on top of her. The heaviest stone weighs 51.4 kilograms. 'He must have been one strong bastard,' Bengt said.

Einar Sjöwall finds no evidence of sexual violence. Even though I've read what he wrote many times over the course of more than a year, still I find that my brain is blocking out some of the information. It suddenly feels like I'm reading the report for the first time. Also, this is the first time I'm able to look closely at the picture. There is just one from the autopsy. It shows Birgitta's face and shoulders in half profile. Her shoulders are so narrow. Her eyebrows so sad. The interrogations seem to suggest that more photos were taken of the autopsy. Someone must have thrown them away.

One Thursday I finally do something I've been planning to do for a long time: I start working on a post for the Perstorp Facebook group. All afternoon, I walk around with Vivi asleep in her carrier, trying out various strings of words in my mind. As long as I keep moving she stays sleeping, so I walk and walk, mile after mile from Lilla Sickla to Söderbysjön, from Skogskyrkogården to Gamla Enskede. That evening, once every word is in its place, Justus gives me the very good advice to wait until the next day to post. I'd just lie awake all night otherwise.

This isn't the first time I've spent time in a 'You know you're from xxx when . . .' sort of Facebook group. I use them to research my walking tours by searching out local stories. But this group doesn't feel like the others. The atmosphere is something else. Previous posts about Birgitta have almost always provoked dismissive or angry replies. One person posted several old clippings about the murder, and one of them included a photo of a boy. *The suspected 14-year-old boy* is written beneath the picture. I can tell from the comments his name had been posted then removed by a moderator. Other posts, which might have made good starting points for discussion, are left untouched. It feels unfamiliar. People tend to be interested in this sort of thing, right? But the citizens of Perstorp are defensive. One person writes that it's insensitive to her relatives to start poking around in that. Is this really about concern for them, or something else? Pain, fear? Loyalty, maybe. But to whom? The Sivander family moved away a very long time ago. Perhaps it is about loyalty to Perstorp as a place; a town where many families have remained for a long time, for generations. I don't know. Perstorp is like a castle with high walls.

My unfinished master's thesis in history was based on accounts of pregnancy and childbirth from women who gave birth between the 1930s and 1960s. The primary sources were questionnaires filled out by women at retirement homes in the early 1990s. Some respondents were dry and matter-of-fact. Others wrote long, incoherent answers. One produced more than ten pages about giving birth, with growing agitation. You could sense it in the handwriting, which became increasingly dense and sloping, the letters smaller and smaller until it was unreadable. Deciphering it, I understood that the woman had suffered years of abuse from her husband.

I felt almost exasperated by another woman who wrote succinctly and without emotion. She skipped every question that might possibly touch on her feelings. My research was concerned with emotional history, so I believed her answers were unusable.

The historian Lynn Abrams's writing about oral history theory changed my mind. I realised how I might be able to read the silences in those stories. Abrams writes that people who have experienced trauma often have difficulty formulating coherent narratives. Trauma can manifest itself as a lack of control over one's emotions, a frenzy of self-expression, but it can also result in its absence. Sociologist Ken Plummer writes that a story about sexual possession or trauma cannot exist without an audience to receive it. This applies to other types of experiences as well.

The story of Birgitta's murder has two families at its centre: Sivander and Sommer. I know from Karl that the Sivander family did not talk about what happened. Karl received no outside support, not from teachers nor from the church. Friends didn't dare to mention it for fear of stirring up unwanted feelings. Karl was told not to speak to journalists. But he had suffered a terrible trauma, and there was no one to tell his story to. This way of handling Birgitta's death rippled from the Sivander family out to the whole of Perstorp. You can still feel it today.

On 14 August I post in the Perstorp Facebook group. I tell them I'm writing about Birgitta's case and ask if anyone would like to speak to me about it. The first response I receive is a private message from a woman telling me she finds it distasteful that I'm writing about this. I ask if there's anything in particular she's afraid of, but she never replies. The second response is from a man saying that previous posts about the murder have been removed, and mine is upsetting people. Then I mostly receive some likes, though not as many as other posts in the group. A few share it.

As a child, I was terrified of ghosts. My grandmother lived next door to the local haunted house. Her back door looked out over it, and her property shared a fence with its garden, which was overgrown and long abandoned. The fence had collapsed and you could enter the lot, which was large. In its middle a large wooden house stood, three storeys plus a basement. Dad told me that when he was little three sisters still lived there. Their father hung himself, and they never married, or moved. They eventually died there, probably sometime in the 1970s.

When I was 8, my older sister suggested we camp out in that abandoned garden with a friend. After dark, my sister started telling us a horrible story about a man turning into a worm. I got so scared that I wanted to go back to Grandma's. But they wouldn't go with me. Finally, I couldn't take it anymore and threw myself into the late summer darkness and ran in a wild panic through Grandma's rose garden and up her stone steps, flung open the door and slammed it shut behind me. In the safely lit hall, I stood with my hands on my knees until able to breathe normally. Then I joined the adults who were drinking wine and watching *Midsomer Murders*, and pretended nothing was wrong.

I was always terrified of the haunted house. But, at the same time, I always wanted to read ghost stories and watch horror movies. People think scary things are for those who aren't afraid. But it's the opposite. They both attract and repel. You need to know your enemy.

Vivi's able to sleep alone now. I keep my back to her and lie beneath my own blanket. It's nice to sleep that way. I haven't done it in eight months. I sleep better. Except those moments when I wake up in terror wondering if she's still alive. Then I creep close to check her warm little body, her regular breath.

One evening when Sam is at his grandmother's, Justus and I stay up late talking. We drink a glass of wine and I tell him about how Vivi is sleeping by herself now. I'm surprised when I start to cry.

'It feels like she's moving away from me,' I say.

'No, it's not that,' he replies.

'You don't understand.'

We were one; she grew inside me. When she emerged she was so helpless, she needed me.

'She still needs you,' he objects.

But the circle is broken. She gets impatient in her carrier during the day, too.

'She just wants to be carried,' I say to anyone who will listen, a patient smile pinned to my face. But I've begun to wonder if I'm the one who needs to carry her. I'm not ready; I want to keep being with her.

I think about what happened to Birgitta's mother. To have carried a child inside you, given birth to her, carried her in your arms. Held her at your breast. The baby blindly searching for your nipple in the night. The two of you, surrounded by darkness, alone inside the light. Imagine if someone were to break that bond.

100

Or was it never like that for Birgitta and her mother? From Karl I learned that Margit was quite strict. He says that after Birgitta's death, she was a grieving mother to the outside world, but cold towards her family. You weren't supposed to speak of the murder, just move on with your life.

Margit passed away a few years ago. When the children were taking care of her estate, they found Birgitta's things. I can see Margit in front of me, sitting there among her lost daughter's cardigans and drawings, deep grooves around the beautiful eyes that Birgitta inherited. How long was she able to breathe in Birgitta's scent with those small clothes pressed to her face? At some point it must have been replaced by the smell of dust and salt.

Vivi and I are on our way home from Lilla Sickla when she makes that noise again. It sounds almost like she's laughing but inwardly and inverted. She's been doing it on and off for a few weeks. We interpreted it as her playing with a new sound, but lately I've started to wonder. It doesn't feel like she's having fun. It seems involuntary. She's sitting in the pushchair. Isn't she a little purple around the mouth? Between her upper lip and her nose. A blue shadow. My heart starts to race. Maybe she's just cold from sitting in the pushchair instead of being pressed against my chest like usual? I call Justus. Ask him to call the national medical information number. If he calls now and gets in the queue, he'll probably reach them right around the time we get home. At that very moment Vivi starts to fuss, and I take her out of the pushchair, put her in the carrier. We're in Björkhagen by Markus church; I rock her and sing quietly: '*The winds whisper into the forests. The rapids roar in the rivers. The waves rock slowly, the waves rock slowly, rock slowly on towards Siljan's shore.*'

When I get home, I trade Vivi for Justus's phone. She protests loudly. An automatic voice tells me I'm next in line to speak to someone. Soon I'm agitatedly telling all this to a nurse while stirring dinner on the stove.

'Is she purple now?'

I go take a look. Vivi is sitting on the sofa with Justus and Sam. She lights up when I arrive, cries heartbrokenly when I leave. I have to walk far away to hear what the nurse is saying.

'No,' I say, 'she looks normal now.'

The nurse isn't worried. But says it's best to get it checked out, of course. She advises me to book a doctor's appointment just in case.

The next day, Justus is with Vivi at the paediatrician and I'm at home. The phone rings, and I pick up immediately.

'Don't freak out,' Justus begins.

My heart starts pounding in my chest. I knew something was wrong.

'But Vivi has a heart murmur. The doctor said it's probably nothing to worry about. They're giving us a referral for a heart ultrasound.'

When they arrive home, I greet Vivi with outstretched arms, and she does the same. I gather her close to me.

'Like I said, it's probably not dangerous at all,' says Justus, 'but it is substantial. You can even hear it if you put your ear to her chest.'

I press my ear to her back and hear rustling. It sounds like the sea inside a shell.

I buy a small figurine at the Red Cross thrift store. It's of a girl reading a book, made in white porcelain. It wasn't particularly striking among all those other knick-knacks, but I bought it anyway. After we get home, I place it in a square niche above the fireplace, and only then do I realise it symbolises Birgitta. I put a green vase next to her, with small-leaved eucalyptus growing inside. It bends over the little girl like a tree. It feels like I've given Birgitta someplace to be safe. I point at her, and Vivi turns her face in that direction.

'Look!' I say.

Vivi waves tentatively at her.

I place two small candles between the girl and the vase. Their light dances warmly across her face.

It's five o'clock and time for the 'quiet hour'. I've introduced it so Vivi can fall asleep more easily at night. From five o'clock on the lights are kept dim. We speak in calm voices and play calm games. Sam gets hushed once every minute. Then Vivi takes her bath.

Tonight, I'm a prisoner, trapped between carrying, feeding, playing, and patiently nodding and listening to Sam's stories about war, ships and monsters. I give Justus a desperate look and tell him I'm headed into the bath first. When the water cools enough, Vivi can join me. I close the door behind me, and I can still hear them, but the sound of the faucet muffles it all. And once I lower my head beneath the surface of the water, I can't hear them at all.

Justus enters the bathroom with Vivi and as soon as she sees me, she stretches her little arms to me and cries out a desperate *Eeeh! Eeeh! Eeeh!* I gather her to me and dip her feet carefully, afraid it still might be too hot. She grimaces a little, but then starts splashing and reaching her hands towards the water. The bathroom door closes, and we're alone, finally. She plays for a while, and I make sure her head stays above water. Periodically she comes back to me, puts a hand on my sternum and says *da*. Then she's off again. She splashes her hands and babbles happily. Heat and steam rise from the water and us, frizzing my hair and making the moisturiser on my face stream down my cheeks.

Justus comes back. He has a large grey towel that came from my childhood home, now rough with age, and wraps her in it. She's slippery as a seal, and we fumble a little. She holds her hands in her lap while he gently dries her. The light on her round little belly is golden. I'm reminded that they too are a unit, not just her and me.

I puncture the scene with one breath as I step out of the tub. I have to hurry to dry off, and when I pick her up Vivi is still warm and steaming like a dumpling. She smells faintly of the same scent-free cream that I use. I have to hold her tight, so she doesn't slip out of my arms. I meet Justus's eyes in the mirror. They're shining, and his face is gentle and soft. I can see that he loves us.

Karl goes down the stairs hesitantly. He's dressed in a light suit and shirt. Downstairs, his family are waiting. Mama and Papa are sitting on either side of the chaise longue, dressed in black. Grandfather Harald stares out the window. Erik, pale and silent, is sitting on the sofa at the other end of the room. Next to him is the nanny, Cecilia. She holds a warning finger up to Karl. He must be quiet. Karl almost expects Birgitta to come bounding down the stairs behind him. He can still feel her there. A wavy strand of hair floating down towards the floor.

His dead little sister has been laid out on the dining-room table. A clock ticks, a candle has been lit. Its flame is completely still. There is no life, no movement around it. Birgitta's face is covered by a white handkerchief. It wasn't possible to paint it beautiful again. No one will see it. But how will he know it's her? Know she's really dead? The early summer sun is shining relentlessly through the window.

'I want to see her face,' Karl declares.

'But Karl,' Mama says.

'You don't want that,' his father adds.

'Yes.' He insists. 'I want to see her.'

They try to convince him that it's not a good idea, without telling him why. Karl stands his ground. In the end, they give in. He lifts the handkerchief.

I didn't recognise her.

Her head, her face had been crushed.

So.

So it was.

It's a cold, clear Monday at the end of November. Vivi's in the pushchair holding her toy cat. Her cheeks and the tip of her nose glow red against her pale skin. We've started walking to the Skogskyrkogården cemetery almost every day. When I was little, we would go there twice a year – once in the summer, to plant flowers, and then on All Saints' Day in November to place heather and light candles. By that time of year it's so dark you stumble almost blindly between the head-stones, the lit candles forming an endless starry sky between the pines and firs. One autumn evening not long after my grandfather's death when I was 16, I went there to visit his grave. I got lost and found no one to ask directions. For hours I walked in circles, until Dad finally tracked me down at the exit to the highway.

Now I know my way around. A straight path, 888 metres long, runs from north to south. A pond lies in front of a chapel of the Holy Cross. On the other side of it, on a slight rise, there stands a rectangular block of stone surrounded by raised torches. Vivi wants to watch the pond ripple in the icy wind, so we go closer. While she's focused on the surface of the water with eyes round and mouth pursed, I look up at the hill with the stone and the torches. Something clicks inside me, and I am engulfed in memory. I can hear Karl telling me about how Birgitta's body was laid out in their home in Perstorp. How he walked over and looked under the white cloth. Why do I think of it now? A wave of sadness and horror washes over me. The stone on that hill is a catafalque. I can see that now. It's a place for a coffin. I think of her lying defenceless against the wind in a thin dress. People walk by us, enjoying the sun. I roll the pushchair up the hill, stand next to the catafalque and extend a hand tentatively. I hold it still in the air for a moment before placing it on the cold, mute stone.

In front of the Forest chapel, I light a candle and place it beside one of the pillars. Despite the wind, the flame burns on steadily. As I stand there watching it, Vivi wakes up and waves at the light. I wave with her, and a shadow slips away and joins the darkness behind the pillars.

That evening I'm lying in bed with an arm around Vivi. She's sleeping peacefully. Soon I'll head downstairs to watch TV with Justus. But it's so warm and comfortable here that I shiver with pleasure, while outside the blanket, it's cold. So I lie there listening to her gentle breathing. Suddenly I feel the bed sink down behind my back. Someone has sat down there, but I didn't hear the door creak. I become afraid and don't move. The presence is so palpable that I expect to touch a silent body if I were to reach out. But I don't dare. I tighten my arm and slowly pull Vivi closer to me. She sighs in her sleep, and I stare hard into the darkness. After a while the weight lifts.

It takes me a few minutes to find the courage to sit up. I look around the room. Faint yellow light from the streetlights 11 floors below us seeps in beneath the blinds. Only after I run my eyes along the walls in search of unfamiliar shadows do I finally get up and head down the stairs. Justus is on the sofa.

'Do you know what just happened?' I say.

'No, what?'

He looks up from his phone.

'There was . . .'

I hesitate.

'I could have sworn somebody came in and sat down behind me on the bed.'

'What?'

'Yeah, I thought it was you at first!'

He looks confused. Then he raises a finger in the air as if he's got the answer.

'You had sleep paralysis.'

'Really? I'm not sure. I wasn't asleep.'

'You *think* you weren't asleep.'

I never fall asleep doing bedtime.

Later I read that people suffering sleep paralysis usually can't move. But I could.

I'm in my study writing when the phone rings. The children's heart clinic has an appointment, tomorrow. Someone has rescheduled. My initial feeling is of relief, but it's quickly replaced by a jolt of anguish in my stomach. Soon we will know. Images flicker before my eyes. Vivi sedated on an operating table built for an adult, a shining knife slicing through the thin skin of her chest, through everything that is sacred. A tiny, white coffin. I *know* it's common for children to have heart murmurs. Very common. But Vivi has a 'substantial murmur'. I want her with me right now.

I shut down my computer, go downstairs and lift her up. I put my ear to her chest, and she pulls at my hair while I listen. I imagine this is how it would sound if you played an organ underwater, hitting two keys one after the other.

At night I dream about her appointment. The doctor applies cold, pool-blue gel to Vivi's chest and then runs the ultrasound wand along her entire torso. Vivi squirms in my arms and gel gets all over us. She spins around, and the doctor follows her contours in confusion. Then the doctor turns off the device, while I try to wipe up the gel. She shows me Vivi's interior on the screen, and it's just one big heart. At the place in her body where the heart should be there's a hole. I hear the rush and hiss of blood flowing back and forth between her right and left side.

I wake up at four o'clock and can't go back to sleep. I doze until seven, then I get up and shower. Sam's in the kitchen eating breakfast. He must sense my anxiety, because he asks if Vivi's going to die. 'No, no,' I answer with a smile and pat his cheek.

At the hospital I take off Vivi's onesie. They keep a heat-lamp in here, so the children won't get too cold. As for me, I'm sweating and dressed too warmly. Vivi leans back on my lap during the exam. The doctor turns off the lights in the room and turns on the children's show *Babblarna*. I sing along with it and move Vivi's arms as the doctor applies ultrasound gel to her chest and glides the wand around. I glance over at the screen trying to interpret what I see. Blue and red pulses against black and white. From a certain angle, the human heart looks just like the heart symbol. The doctor is silent. What does that mean? After a quarter of an hour it's over, luckily, since Vivi's out of patience. The doctor looks at the ultrasound pictures while I get her dressed. She hands me paper towels, and I wipe off the gel as best I can before putting Vivi's navy blue onesie back on. I kiss her cheek, bury my nose in her soft neck.

'Vivi has a hole in the bottom of her heart,' the doctor says.

I nod slowly into Vivi's unconcerned head and study the doctor's face. I can't read her. Her expression seems mild, is that compassion? Tiny white coffins and weathered stuffed animals on cold earth flicker before my eyes. I wrap my arms around Vivi, as if the doctor were threatening to take her from me. I stop breathing.

'But that doesn't affect how the heart works. It all looks fine. I think she must have looked blue because she was cold. Come back when she's 3, and we'll take another look. Maybe it will have grown over by then.'

I sob while she shows it to me on the screen. The image reminds me of that first ultrasound, when Vivi was in my stomach. There's an ache in my forehead, in my throat and behind my breastbone, as if there were three large dams inside me, each ready to burst.

I thank the doctor repeatedly and say Merry Christmas, even though it's only early December. When I reach the hallway, I slide down onto the floor with my back against the wall. For a long time I just rock my healthy baby, and she coos in response until she gets impatient and starts struggling to get free. I don't spare a thought for the parents who might have received a death sentence in the room we just left. I go to the hospital's gift shop and search for a present for Vivi, for being healthy. I end up buying an overpriced rabbit almost as big as her. We take a taxi home. Then she falls asleep with her hand on the rabbit's ear.

That evening the wind blows so hard the window frames rattle and ash swirls out of the open fireplace. I stand at the window and watch the pine trees sway like unsteady drunks. I take a deep breath and let it out slowly. In my head I kneel down before golden temples and lit torches, before every god, in gratitude for my daughter, sleeping peacefully on the floor above, alive.

Vivi has five teeth breaking through at the same time and has just started walking. She staggers forward through life with her slightly more stable left foot first, her arms and fingers making soft upward arcs, groping for something to hang on to. She walks gently in the moss, carefully circling around hard stones, supports herself with her hand against a tree. I walk backwards in front of her with outstretched hands, luring her towards me. She keeps walking because she thinks she'll reach my arms soon. At first she laughs, then she starts to cry and lies down hopeless on her stomach with her face pressed to the ground.

You fail your children every day. Tiny betrayals of their boundless trust. You do it out of love, trying to find the balance between letting go and holding on. But no matter what I do, I feel like I'm getting it wrong. I hold too tight or go too far away. I want to leave and stay close. It never ends up right.

In the evening, I lie in the death pose on my yoga mat in the study with my headphones on, trying to block out the sounds from downstairs. Today we're doing a relaxation exercise. The yoga instructor mentions different body parts fairly quickly. I silently repeat what she says, like an echo. Left thumb, left forefinger, left middle finger, left ring finger, left little finger. The palm of your hand. The top of the hand. The wrist. The forearm. My thoughts drift. I think of Birgitta.

When we've gone through the whole body, we do it again. Then again and again. The nerves are starting to respond. My hair stands on end. I become aware of my body parts and their endpoints, like a star. Waves of energy sweep through my arms and legs, stomach, back. Across my eyelids and forehead and through my eyebrows and over my cheeks. I close my eyes. Then something happens – a light turns on in the corner. It's a solar-powered lamp that we bought at Ikea when we moved here. But it never worked, just stood there with dust slowly accumulating on it. I break position and sit up to look beneath the shade. The diode is sharp and white. I perceive a movement to the right of the lamp. That's where my headphone case is sitting. I can see that the tab of its zipper is moving, swinging back and forth. I take off my headphones. It becomes quiet, except for Sam's and Justus's distant voices. I stare at the zipper for a few seconds, then grab hold of it to stop it. Then I stare at it to see if it will start swinging again. But it's still. When I return to the death pose and close my eyes, the light is still on. The next time I open my eyes, it's out.

After Sam is dropped off at preschool, we climb into the car – Justus, Vivi and I – and drive to Liljeholmskajen. The city archive has opened a new branch there, containing, among other things, the 1938 birth records.

Vivi is asleep in her car seat, as I jump out of the car and cross the street in the rain. Inside the building it's so quiet that it feels like you've covered your ears. I go over to the information desk and say, 'I'm looking for a girl.' Not a maternity record. A solitary young man is sitting there. Their computer system is down, and he doesn't know how to find the archives without it. I sigh and go to the reading room to write a little. Maybe it will start up again soon. After a while, a bearded man pokes his head in.

'Is it maternity records for '38 you're looking for? Which month?'

'August.'

He comes back soon with the right tome. I've found her.

Margit is 22 years old when she enters the clinic early in the morning on 20 August. The full moon's just dipped below the horizon and been replaced by a red sun rising on the other side of the city. The baby's head has descended deep into her pelvis. The contractions started at ten o'clock the previous evening. Margit is given anaesthetic gas. Some fifteen minutes later, the bearing-down contractions begin, and after another quarter of an hour, at five o'clock in the morning, Birgitta is born with the amniotic membrane intact. For a few seconds, those present can see Birgitta as she looked in her mother's womb. Being born with the membrane intact on the head is also called being born with a caul. It's unusual, and even more unusual to be born with a fully intact amniotic membrane.

It's considered a good omen. According to folk tales, children born with a caul were protected from stabbing, beating and drowning. They could be gifted with second sight as well. The membranes were sometimes dried and worn around the child's neck. In the Swedish Royal Armoury, Karl XII's caul has been preserved. His sister, Ulrika Eleonora the Younger, took care of it after he was shot in the head in 1718 and died, aged 36. It didn't protect him. Ulrika Eleonora was also born with a caul, and that too now resides at the Royal Armoury. She wore it inside a piece of jewellery as a protective amulet, and died of smallpox at the age of 53 in 1741. Some folk beliefs about the magical powers of the caul probably still lingered when Birgitta was born, but her parents were rational people, and didn't save it.

Birgitta weighs 3.6 kilograms and is 52 centimetres long. Margit is bleeding heavily. That's not surprising considering how quickly it took place. Mother and daughter are kept at the maternity hospital for ten days, in a room they share with four other mothers.

Now I know what time of day Birgitta was born, out of curiosity I enter her time of birth into an astrology website. It measures the position of the stars and calculates the houses of her horoscope. One website says she has Aries in the eighth house – the house that supposedly reveals how you'll die. The presence of Aries there can foretell a sudden death, possibly from violent injuries to the head or brain. And in her midheaven sign is a star called Algol. The demon star. It represents beheading, injuries to the back of the head and neck, murder, violence, disaster and evil. Blood and death.

Reading this, the hair rises on the back of my arms. After a moment's hesitation, I check which signs are in my eighth house. Libra and Virgo. Undramatic, quiet, something to do with digestion, says Virgo. Maybe related to the kidneys, says Libra. I exhale and close the computer.

The woods around Perstorp are full of children. They've been given time after the morning recess to pick flowers for the funeral. Lilies of the valley. They jump over rocks and streams, whisper and squabble about the flowers. Now each class heads down towards the church. Dressed in white, they line up along both sides of the road. When the Sivander family climb out of their car, the scent of thousands of small white flowers washes over them. Six girls, Birgitta's classmates, grab hold of the coffin's handles and lift it up. The other children stand like a protective wall between the procession and the adults towering behind them. Serious, curious eyes follow the coffin. The family walk behind, eyes lowered. It takes a long time for them to make their way there, and everything seems dreamlike and misty. The child standing closest to the church, the forester's son, is holding the school's banner which is draped with black crepe. He lowers his head as the family pass by him and go through the church doors.

Inside it's packed. The pews creak as people fidget anxiously, and the occasional clearing of the throat or sob echoes inside. The Sivander family walk in a line down the aisle. The congregation watches them with glistening eyes as they approach the empty pew at the front. Margit, Valdemar, Grandfather Harald, Karl and Erik. Eva is at home with the nanny. The coffin at the front is white and unusually small. The children's choir waits nervously for the signal, the first notes from the organ, to begin the funeral with Birgitta's favourite song – 'The Flowers' Prayer'.

119

Do you think little flowers pray to God?
Even though you can't hear a sound,
yet up to the sky from the meadow green
the prayer of the flowers rises so slowly.
Be like the flower, rejoice and sing,
praise the Mighty on High, when you are young!

Don't all the flowers stretch upwards
their little heads, brim and bud?
Sweet and still is their song.
Listen to the sound of the bluebells ring!
Be like the flower, rejoice and sing,
praise the Mighty on High, when you are young!

Don't all the flowers bend now?
They must be tired, don't you think?
No, just humbly they bow now,
praising their Creator softly.
Be like the flower, rejoice and sing,
praise the Mighty on High, when you are young!

Their clear voices ring out beneath the arches. When the children's choir falls silent, it's the adults' turn to take part in this rite. The priest has chosen hymn number 355, 'Day by Day (and with Each Passing Moment)'. Then verses 7–8 of hymn number 283. *Like small birds when thunder sounds and beasts are frightened, they scatter from danger.*

The men's voices are bass, the women's, shrill sopranos.

The priest takes his place in front of the coffin and clasps his hands. He looks down for a few seconds, then raises his face to the congregation and begins his funeral oration.

'We are horrified, and we have gathered in front of this bier with endless questions: why? Why? It's so cruel and senseless.'

He turns to Valdemar and Margit.

'Your beloved daughter Birgitta was a ray of sunshine who chased away the shadows in your home, and among her peers she was truly a child of light, bright and warm to those she touched. This tender flower has been cut; her young petals have fallen to the cold and darkness of the world. But your flower will bloom again in heaven where there is no cold and no darkness, where warmth and light are eternal.'

The mourners walk home through the scent of lilies of the valley; it saturates their clothes. It will always remind them of death.

On Friday 8 May 2015, a lid is lifted at the cemetery in Perstorp. A tube with two urns inside is exposed. Karl glances over at the white one, which belongs to Birgitta. It looks exactly the same as it did when it was lowered here 67 years ago, as if time stopped beneath the earth. Her father, Valdemar, has been resting next to her for 50 years. Now her mother, Margit, is going to join them.

The tube was installed so that it could be reopened and the urns moved. No one could imagine the Sivander family staying in Perstorp after the murder. When they moved, they'd lift the lid, pluck out the white urn and take Birgitta with them. That was why she was cremated – so she could travel with her family when they left. But that's not how it happened. Valdemar applied for jobs elsewhere, but nothing ever came of it. The Sivander family stayed in Perstorp until Valdemar's death, almost twenty years after the murder. Finally, Margit moved away. It must have been a relief; afterwards, she blossomed.

I'm standing with my eyes fixed on the tiles above the stove, shaking a frying pan so the meatballs won't burn, when suddenly I see Margit in front of me. The image is created by my intense curiosity about how it would have felt to share a small town like Perstorp with the family whose son might have murdered your daughter.

I see Margit as clearly as if I had a projector on my forehead and the tiles were a white screen. She's crossing the square in Perstorp when she sees Rut Sommer. Rut's eyes glare at Margit like burning coals, smouldering inside their sockets. Margit's stomach jumps to her chest in both anger and pity. She grabs her purse with both hands, and they stare at each other for a moment. Then Margit turns on her heel and walks in the opposite direction, away from the grocery store. A dark green coat hangs off Rut's thin, hanger-like frame. Her cheekbones are prominent, her eyes too big, fringed by shadows. Margit shakes her head and shuts her eyes tightly. She walks quickly and meets no one's gaze on her way. The rain starts to whip against her face, and it feels like a relief.

The sounds of the meatballs sizzling disappears as I imagine what I would do if I were Margit. If it were Vivi found dead in a ditch. I am walking over asphalt, crossing gravel. Then gravel becomes forest.

Tall, wet grass brushes against my ankles, my thin stockings start to cling. It's cold and uncomfortable, but soon they're the same temperature as my skin. Birch branches hit me in the face, and I take the blows with my eyes closed and mouth open. My purse slips from my grasp, and my hands clench. The energy that has been restrained inside my body needs a way out, and I punch and kick it away. Then I fall forward.

My mouth fills with dirty water, and I struggle wildly as if fighting an invisible enemy. I turn onto my back. The rain falls harder. I stare up at the treetops and a leaden sky. The clouds rush by at an unnatural pace. I exhale what's left in my lungs and don't breathe in again. Instead, I turn back over so I'm lying on my stomach. The stomach that was my daughter's home is pushed into brown water. I want to breathe in that water, fill my lungs with it, pass through it and come out the other side. In reality, my throat and lungs are burning as I hold my breath, like a sacrifice, standing in front of the stove. What would I be willing to do for my daughter?

Tears drip into the frying pan as I see Vivi's lifeless face in front of me. Could I live in a world where she no longer exists? I cup my hands and push them beneath the surface, lift her up, cover her cheeks in kisses. I push myself to the bottom, embracing the roots and leaves, going blind. On the other side are sun-warmed skin, soft hair, the scents of clean cotton clothes, milk and bread. I bury my nose behind Vivi's ears, in her neck, tickle her belly and wrap my arms around her, pressing my lips to her head. Bright stars shine there.

The sound on my computer doesn't work so I restart it. Every program I have running reopens. Suddenly, the entire screen is filled with the image of Birgitta, dead on the autopsy table. It wasn't there before. I turn my face away and close my eyes. When I open them again, she's still there. I try to close the window, but it doesn't work, the computer screen is frozen. I contemplate Birgitta's face. Remembering the first time I saw this picture at the archive in Lund. Back then I thought it didn't look so bad, not quite as awful as I had feared. Now I am horrified.

'Remember why you're doing this,' she says. 'It's because someone did this to me.'

Part Two
Let Me In

Alone it slithers in rings,
feeling both wicked and foul,
high above the lark swings,
floats along on joyous wings
listen now, hear it sing,
where serpents are not allowed.

Gustaf Fröding, 'The Serpent's Song'

I wake up as Birgitta's hand slips from mine. Sam bursts in, needs help blowing his nose. I ask Sam to go grab some tissues. He misunderstands, thinks I'm telling him to blow his nose by himself. He says 'Okay' unhappily and closes the door. I put my head back on the pillow and close my eyes. Maybe if I fall asleep again, she'll come back to me, but she doesn't. The next time I wake up, I wonder if my grief for this strange girl is affecting my own children.

The whole family have been home sick for a while now. Vivi doesn't understand what's happening inside her and wants to be pressed against my body around the clock. Sam's been home from preschool for more than a week. He's climbing the walls in frustration and needs our attention constantly. Every conversation sounds something like this:

'Wanna see, Mummy?'

'Not now, Sam.'

The look of dejection on his face is heartbreaking. Yesterday I asked:

'What if Daddy takes care of Vivi tomorrow, and you and I hang out just us?'

He'd smiled and said how much he'd like that.

'We can go to the trench!'

Sam has been telling us stories about an imaginary kingdom called Telefonia since he was 3. It seems to be mostly based on the Roman Empire. Every historical titbit he picks up joins the patchwork of Telefonia.

Near our flat there's a small, brush-covered hill. It was once an Iron Age burial ground, but now there sits a huge concrete square atop it – the foundation of a giant searchlight that could shine a kilometre into the sky. They used it during World War II to search for incoming bombers during the blackouts. It must have felt so strange, to stand next to the only source of light in a pitch-black city.

We head there now, and I wind through the bushes behind Sam, climbing over fallen trees and dead brushwood. He points to where the bombs fell on Telefonia, then to a prison where some three thousand people were once locked up, all of it on this hill. 'Look, Mum, you know what that is? That's a Nazi rifle, cut down the middle. Do you see it?' I do.

'And look there, you see that circle?'

'What, where?'

Sam, in red mittens, points with one hand while holding a trowel in the other. It's for excavations, because he's an archaeologist.

'On the ground, over there.'

My field of vision blackens around the edges. There in the mud, old twigs have been trampled aside to form a circle, like an iris without a pupil. My son, with muddy overalls and red cheeks, is transformed into a forester in a tangled wood some five hundred kilometres away. How could he know that my head is full of circles, earth that's been trampled into this shape? Can he read my mind? He's still pointing, urging me.

'Yes . . . No,' I say uncertainly.

He pauses for a moment, then points to the narrow opening and says impatiently:

'There! Come on, you can fit through there!'

He starts walking. I don't want to play this game anymore.

'You go on, I have to go out.'

'No!'

'It's okay, I'll be able to see you from outside. You go play.'

'No, Mummy, no!'

When I exit the bushes, the wind is blowing colder. I pull my coat tighter around me. His tiny form is just barely visible through dense branches. He's standing with his back to me, and I can hear him crying. He slowly starts walking further away from me.

'Stop Sam, I can't see you there!'

But he's sad and hurt and keeps going. Suddenly I'm afraid. What if he disappears, what if someone's waiting for my unattended child inside the forest?

'I'm coming, stay where you are!'

I have to walk all the way around the bushes to get back inside. I can't see him. Anxiety blurs my vision, and the branches whip into my face, a just punishment for a woman who abandons her child. I can feel my tears in my throat, each one a sharp stone I have swallowed. I push through twigs with my palms pressed together as if in prayer.

Then I see him. The muddy overalls, the striped hat that has slipped down to his eyelashes. He's crying so hard his shoulders shake, and I sink down into the mud and wrap my arms around him. We cry together. I feel like I have brought him back from the edge. After that I play trenches with him for two more hours, out of guilt and relief.

It's St Lucy's Day. I load Vivi into the baby carrier for a walk, hoping to get her to sleep. The weather's grey and raw outside, and we haven't seen the sun since the beginning of December. By four o'clock we're home again, just finishing our rice pudding and about to bring out the mulled wine and saffron buns, when Vivi starts to cry.

'Could she be tired already?' Justus wonders.

I ask him to brush her teeth and put on her pyjamas; we'll see how she does after that. He brings her in five minutes later. She's still fussing. When I lie down next to her, she falls silent.

Even when she has fallen asleep, she can't seem to settle. She scratches and grabs at my cheeks, my neck, my ears, my arms. Just when I think she's about to fall into a deeper sleep, she's startled awake again and starts to howl. It's impossible. I feel like I'm losing my mind. Like this will never end. I put a headphone in one ear and turn on a podcast. To keep from moving any more than necessary, I press play on the first thing that comes up, a true crime documentary about the murder of Engla Höglund. I stare intently into the darkness, while Vivi grows heavy on my arm. Engla was murdered 60 years after Birgitta. But as each parallel arises between the two cases, chills run down my spine. Birgitta was almost ten, Engla had just turned ten. They were murdered in the spring – Birgitta on 7 May, Engla on 5 April. Birgitta was last seen hanging around a football field before her murder, as was Engla. Engla's mother speaks in the documentary about how her daughter called her and asked to bike home. She had hesitated, because her daughter

132

didn't have a helmet, but she gave in. I think of Birgitta's long bike ride, and the words 'five kilometres' pop into my mind the second before they're said on the radio; Engla's ride home was the same distance. I can see the search party in 1948 and the search party in 2008, as if layered on top of each other, making their way through a dark forest.

From the testimony of Constable Ivar Björk:

Chairman: How would you describe Bengt's demeanour when you picked him up and during the questioning?

Björk: A little anxious, but otherwise he was calm and collected.

[. . .]

Chairman: Did he seem to be unaffected by the crime?

Björk: Yes, you could put it like that. You'd expect a boy in that situation to act differently. [. . .] He seemed mostly concerned with missing the football match. [. . .]

Chairman: He denied going down the forest road. Were those denials very definite?

Björk: Yes, they were. We told him there was a witness who had seen him, but he still denied it strongly.

Chairman: How long did he continue to deny it?

Björk: It was our opinion that since he refused to admit to it, we needed to bring in Oskarsson as soon as possible to meet with the boy.

I rewind time, and suddenly I see him. The boy is tugging at his collar, which tightens around his neck. A stubborn cowlick sticks straight up at the front of his blonde hair. It was ten o'clock on Sunday morning when Edvin Oskarsson walked into the police station to report seeing Bengt Sommer walking towards the forest. From that moment on, it's been as if a spotlight has been turned on Bengt. The brightness of its beam makes it difficult to see anything outside of its perimeters.

'I was in the changing room when I noticed Birgitta Sivander and another young woman near the entrance,' Edvin had told them. 'I could see them through the window.' During the interview, Senior Constable Magnusson asked why he was in the changing room. Edvin explained he was there to check on some team shirts, to see if they needed washing or not. He washed his hands afterwards, and so he ended up standing at the sink. No one asks how he got his hands dirty looking at some jerseys. 'Less than five minutes before or after that, I noticed Bengt Sommer in the middle of the road that heads through the forest to the dump. He glanced around, then jogged in the direction of the dump.'

At approximately the same time, Edvin reported that he saw a group of boys playing football on the old field. He thought Bengt might be headed up into the forest in order to come down again and scare them. About half an hour later, Edvin left the football field and biked to Assar Andersson's to pay a bill for some hauling services, before travelling on along

Köpmangatan, to Café Centrum, where he stayed for around fifteen minutes.

It's now almost six o'clock on Sunday evening. Senior Constable Magnusson and Constable Björk spent hours tracking down Edvin Oskarsson. They wanted to bring him in to talk with the boy, who continues stubbornly to deny having gone anywhere other than home after being at the football fields. Still, he also has difficulty explaining why he arrived home so late and why his shoes were so muddy. Surely he'd be more likely to confide in his coach than in a couple of police officers?

The door to the interrogation room opens. Inside, Bengt is sitting all alone, slumped over in a chair. Edvin is waved inside and settles down opposite Bengt. He leans across the table, and the legs of his chair scrape against the floor as he pulls it closer.

'Hi, Bengt . . .' the officers hear him say before closing the door and leaving the man alone with the boy.

Later, after Edvin goes home for dinner, the door to the interrogation room opens again. Bengt is still sitting in the same place. Now Constable Björk returns accompanied by another man.

'This is Mr Sven Ekvall, chairman of the Perstorp Child Welfare Board,' explains Constable Björk.

Ekvall grabs a chair from the corner and sits down next to Bengt.

'Hi there, Bengt,' the man says, then turns to the constable. 'Bengt and I already know each other. He's one of my students at Central school.'

Constable Björk nods, uninterestedly, and takes out a pen and paper to begin the interrogation.

'So, do you have anything new to tell us, Bengt? Edvin Oskarsson says you just admitted to him you didn't go straight home, like you previously stated. You actually went to the dump.'

Bengt, eyes downcast, sits there for a long time, then finally gives a slight nod.

'And why did you go there?'

'I was collecting cigarette stamps. Went to see if I could find any.'

'Right.'

Constable Björk takes notes. Bengt tries to see what he's writing, but the constable notices and shields the pad with his left hand.

'How long did you stay there?'

'Ten minutes maybe.'

'And that's where you got your shoes dirty, like your mother told me.'

'Yeah. I think so.'

The constable's pen scratches against the paper. Mr Ekvall crosses one leg over the other and lights a cigarette.

'Do you know what time you got home?'

'It was about eight fifteen.'

'And your mother scolded you.'

'Well, not exactly. I told her I got my shoes dirty, and she said I'd have to clean them off myself.'

'And you did. Did you use only a brush, or did you use water as well?'

'Both a brush and water, just outside the kitchen door.'

Constable Björk continues taking notes for a few seconds, then puts down his pen and meets Bengt's gaze.

'You know it doesn't look good that you lied to us earlier, Bengt. Why did you do that?'

Bengt is sitting on his hands.

'I was afraid you'd think I had something to do with the murder. Think I was up in the forest to murder Birgitta.'

'And you didn't?'

'No!'

Bengt says it more quietly than he intended. He does his best to steadily maintain his gaze into the constable's eyes, to signal that he's telling the truth. Constable Björk sighs.

'Very well, Bengt. Now you can go with Mr Ekvall. He's taking you to Andersson, the parish constable.'

'Can't I go home?'

'No, Bengt. You can't.'

The next day is a Saturday. I take the children to a playground just a few minutes from home. It's oddly quiet, even though it's far from deserted. My phone rings as I open our lunch bag. I answer and hear nothing but silence for a moment or two, then a man on the other end introduces himself in a Skåne accent and tells me that he saw my Facebook post; he's from Perstorp. His father was Sven Ekvall, the chairman of the Child Welfare Board. He tells me he was good friends with Karl until the murder. He misses him and asks if I'm in contact with him. The man speaks quickly, as if he'd taken a deep breath before calling. I curse the fact that I don't have a pen and paper with me. I listen while stopping Vivi from eating fistfuls of gravel. We agree I'll call him back on Monday at four o'clock.

On Sunday, I walk for hours with Vivi in the baby carrier trying to get her to sleep as long as possible. 'Sleep begets sleep,' they like to say. And unfortunately, it's true. If she doesn't sleep long enough during the day, the nights are hell. We walk to Björkhagen. I rub her back and hum while thinking about the man who called me. Maybe he's a link to Birgitta, maybe he can tell me about her. The sun reflects off a bronze sculpture, at the point where you turn to get to Markus church. I've started going there to light candles several times a week. The sculpture depicts a mother, voluminous and soft, playing with her round, healthy child like a kitten with a ball of yarn. The light it reflects blinds me, and I close my eyes as I pass by and enter the small road that leads to the church. It's only then I sense it, for the first time in my waking hours – a tiny hand slipping into mine.

Entering the church is like stepping into a large cave. Out of the raw and gusty air, in through a tall door, you pass by thick walls and enter cool darkness beneath a high ceiling. The lanterns above seem to float. I head to a black metal tree crowned with a large candle. On the branches there are many openings for smaller candles. Together we choose one and light it. I ask her where she wants me to place it. She points silently to a spot close to the big candle. She wants it where it's safest, brightest and warmest. I stare at it for a while.

Then I squeeze my eyes shut tight. I can't allow myself to feel this presence, I can't allow myself to believe this is Birgitta. She doesn't belong to me. I am coming too close to something, some precipice inside me. This grief isn't mine.

The damp chill continues on into Monday. I prepare for my conversation with Sven Ekvall's son by reading through my research again. His father's name appears several times, both in the police investigation and in newspaper articles about the murder. Sven Ekvall was the chairman of the Child Welfare Board in Perstorp in the late 1940s. He was present at several of Bengt's interrogations, as well as discussions about the boy with the police, lawyers and psychologists.

The meetings seemed endless. It's ironic that an organisation whose purpose was to ensure the best interests of the child contributed so much uncertainty to Bengt's life. When an adult is accused of a crime, there's a trial, and then they're either set free or sentenced. But because Bengt was a minor and therefore couldn't formally be accused, he didn't receive a legal trial – though the media referred to the hearing as such anyway. The Child Welfare Board was officially acting in his *best interest*, meaning he remained in their clutches regardless of the outcome of the hearing. And in the 1940s, factors such as poverty, soiled clothing, having a single parent or even the ill will of neighbours could lead to the forced removal of a minor.

A surprising amount of the investigation's file consists of letters from the public. Almost none of these letters suggest Bengt is the killer. Among all the words from the wise, the opinionated or children impersonating a murderer in wobbly handwriting, there are two letters that argue for Bengt Sommer's innocence in a way that implies Ekvall's opinion must have been the opposite. I'm confused by that. In the investigation notes and newspaper articles, Sven Ekvall seems convinced of Bengt's innocence. In *Stockholms-Tidningen*, for example, Ekvall 'emphasises that the suspect has been well behaved, kept up at school, and that he's been a lively and athletic boy, one that's hard to imagine capable of something so evil'. However, Ekvall's son has a very different sense of what his father thought. Over a scratchy phone line, he tells me that his father was fairly sure Bengt was guilty.

'There were those washed clothes, which spoke volumes,' he says. 'You know about those, don't you? The bloodstains?'

Bengt's clothing was initially examined by the coroner, Einar Sjöwall. This was not his area of expertise, but he looked at the clothes early on because of the urgency of the case and found marks there that resembled bloodstains. Professor Sjöwall believed one of the stains appeared to have been washed. Characteristically for the investigation, it immediately became an established truth that these were new bloodstains that someone tried to wash away. But when answers eventually came from the technicians in Stockholm, they showed the stains were old and made by very small amounts of blood.

I decide to change the subject. I ask Ekvall's son if he remembers the funeral.

'Yes, absolutely . . .' he replies, but like Karl, his memories seem to dissolve into nothing.

I wonder if mention of the funeral reignites some of the shock, confusion and grief that every child in Perstorp must have felt in 1948. Emotions they had no words for back then, nor any room to express. I ask Ekvall's son if his father ever talked about the case. He tells me his father never said a word. 'But it weighed on him heavily, very heavily.' After the trial was completed, Sven Ekvall couldn't stand Perstorp. He resigned and moved the family to another town.

Since Birgitta died, everything's been different, but also the same. Karl can see and feel the difference, but no one else at home even acknowledges it. Papa has transformed into a heavy, grey shadow, but he still goes to work every day. Mama has turned hard. Cecilia looks scared all the time, but she keeps making sandwiches, singing nursery rhymes and combing hair. Erik seems confused and somehow younger than before. The only one who's exactly the same is Eva. Karl goes to school. He feels as though there's an invisible fence around him. It's so tangible you can feel it when you stretch out your hand. No one asks him how he is. No one mentions his sister.

It's a Saturday morning, and Karl is standing at the top of the stairs, hesitant to go down. He has a new habit of pausing at the top step to listen. He tries to sense the atmosphere down below. Now he hears his father sighing deeply from inside the kitchen.

'What is it?' his mother says dryly after a few seconds.

'Another letter. It was delivered yesterday. But I just opened it.'

Karl can hear his mother pull out a chair and sit down. 'And what does it say?'

Valdemar starts reading aloud, and Karl quietly takes two steps down the stairs.

'*From a newspaper item on the ninth of May . . . which I find a bit comical . . .*'

Valdemar stops. It's badly written. He reads the line once more, but the result is the same, because that's what it says.

'Comical?' says Margit. 'Ha.'

Valdemar continues reading.

'. . . *a bit comical, if you read this column. It seems quite strange to me that the forester was able to find the girl's* . . .'

Valdemar pauses a moment.

'. . . *the girl's body* . . . *when it was buried under* . . . *a fifty-kilo stone and the like. If you closely examine his photo in this newspaper, he looks like he had something to do with it.*'

'Oh please, dear . . .'

'*As you can see* – "see" has been underlined – *in the photo, he looks like he's thinking that it can never be discovered, how he's the one who did it.*'

'Throw it away, Valdemar.'

'*So I think you should ask the prosecutor to find out where he was on Friday at the time of the murder,*' Valdemar continues.

Karl can hear a chair scraping loudly and quickly against the floor.

'Do you want coffee?'

His mother starts rattling pots and pans. But Valdemar continues relentlessly.

'*I told many of my friends that I am convinced he has something to do with it.*'

'Well, I guess that settles it,' Margit says ironically. 'Is it signed?'

'No, it just says *I'd like to remain anonymous for the time being.*'

Karl has a sinking feeling inside when he hears how tired Papa sounds. He makes his way silently back up the stairs before descending again with loud, heavy steps. The voices in the kitchen fall silent. Karl enters wearing a forced smile.

'I thought I'd go out for a while,' he says as nonchalantly as possible.

The letter is gone now. Probably under the table, in Papa's hands. Mama wipes something invisible off her skirt and walks over to him. She pushes his hair down, so it ends up in his eyes.

'You need a haircut.'

Before he closes the door behind him, he hears his father's voice, a tinge of worry in it.

'Come home for dinner.'

Karl walks past Birgitta's red bicycle without looking at it. With his eyes fixed straight ahead, he walks out the gate. Åke, Yngve and Bittie are out in their yard. Yngve and Bittie run inside when they see Karl. Åke stays, tentatively waving over the hedge. Karl waves back, but doesn't stop. He continues down the street and turns up towards the football field. He hears conversations falling silent around him and feels eyes staring into his back. Everyone knows who he is. Everyone knows he's the older brother of the girl who was murdered.

Karl heads up into the forest. Pine cones and bilberry twigs push their way into his sandals. The familiar sounds of footballs being kicked and kids running and shouting can be heard from the football field. Karl slows down. He runs his hands lightly over the rough tree trunks as he passes by them. Soon he'll be out of sight from everyone. Karl stops and takes a deep breath. The sun meets his face. It's warm, but not hot – soft, gentle. He closes his eyes, and the world turns blood red.

Karl is at the ditch now. Below him is where his sister lay. The lilies of the valley are in full bloom, and their sweet scent in the warmth almost makes Karl nauseous. He drops to his knees, careful not to get bilberry stains on his clothes. He stares down into the ditch, thinking of Birgitta. He can almost hear her voice. A shiver runs down his spine. Then he stands up and heads to a tree right next to the ditch. He grabs on to a branch and starts to climb upwards. His movements contain no hesitation; he goes here almost every day. Now Karl is settled near the top of the tree, his feet against a branch and one arm around the trunk. After he finds a secure seat, he stays where he is. He watches the ditch.

A woodpecker is knocking on a trunk, two squirrels race around another, but the animals avoid his tree. They know it's occupied by another creature. The swallows play above him. Karl watches them. After a while, it looks like they are dancing. The sky is a soft blue. Then an interruption arrives, Karl feels it before he sees it. A hawk. Its wings are straight, and it hovers in the air, watching the swallows. Then it lunges, making a wide arc towards one of them. The hawk misses the swallow and carries on like nothing happened, as if it were just passing by.

Noise approaches. Two men speak softly to each other as they step over heather and bilberry bushes, winding between birches and firs. They stop at the ditch and stare down.

'This is where she was found,' one says to the other.

Karl turns ice cold. He's been waiting for him to show up. The murderer. His friend's older brother told him once that a murderer always returns to the scene of the crime. Since the morning after they found Birgitta dead, he's known it's his duty as her older brother to solve the murder. It was his fault she died; he never should have taken her bike. Birgitta came down to the football field to get it back, and if he hadn't borrowed it, she'd be alive. She might have whizzed past her murderer on the bike, completely unaware she was passing close by her own death. The guilt is heavy on him.

The men mumble to each other down below. They climb down into, then out of the ditch. Karl can't hear what they're saying, but he takes careful note of their appearance and clothing. One is as gaunt as a skeleton, with scraggy yellow hair. He's wearing a thin poplin jacket and dark brown pants. The other man looks athletic, well built, with reddish curls under a flat cap, and a dark grey gabardine suit. Now they squat down, silent. They touch the leaves in the ditch. Are they searching for something? Something they might have lost that evening? An eternity goes by before they get up and leave.

When Karl is sure they're out of earshot, he slides down the trunk and follows the men.

They're walking out of the forest. Karl creeps from tree to tree, pressing his hands against the bark while keeping an eye on them. The men head down the road towards the town. There are quite a few people out and about. Karl casually looks the other way, but he continues down the same road, watching the men out of the corner of his eye. In town they enter the pub. Karl stays on the other side of the street. Through the window he can see the men sitting down at a table, ordering food, eating. Karl switches his weight from foot to foot. He's not sure what he should do. He hasn't thought this part through. Should he dash to the police station and tell them what he saw? But what did he actually see, what would he say? His parents will find out what he's been up to if he reports this to the police. He's picked up a loose thread, but he can't pull on it. Karl tells no one what he's seen.

Sam was born before the child health centre started screening fathers for post-partum depression, but I knew something was wrong. Whenever I handed Sam over to Justus, I felt an anxiety I couldn't explain. I was dizzy and nauseous from exhaustion, but still I couldn't sleep. The wall was only a thin barrier between the bed and the crying, and I heard no comforting sounds coming from Justus. When I went into the room, Sam would be sitting in the baby bouncer, eyes staring into space, while Justus rocked it rhythmically with his foot, his eyes glued to the television. A few times a day I would nag Justus to actually watch Sam.

When Sam was still inside me, I went out once with Justus and his friends. I stood in a corner, with a non-alcoholic beer in my hand. One of Justus's friends, Fredrik, came over to me. I got the feeling that he wanted to talk to someone sober. Or, maybe he saw something was troubling Justus? Was he trying to warn me? One of their mutual friends had committed suicide earlier that year. Fredrik always waved his arms frantically while he spoke, punching the air to emphasise what he had to say: you have to talk to your friends, you have to ask them how they're really doing, you have to tell them how you really feel.

It's Monday.

'Take off your shirt, too.'

Bengt pulls his shirt over his head and stands half naked in the cold room.

'Now stretch out your arms.'

A doctor twists and turns Bengt's pale arms. Constable Björk and Senior Constable Magnusson are standing against the wall, their hands stuffed into their pockets, watching all of it.

'There's a wound on the left.'

The doctor takes out a ruler.

'About forty millimetres long, the scab was formed a while ago.'

Constable Björk notes all this on his pad.

'Where did this come from, Bengt?' the doctor says without meeting his eyes.

'In shop class, last Friday.'

Constable Björk lifts the pen from the paper and stares at him encouragingly. Bengt understands he's supposed to say more.

'I was helping Åke build a rabbit hutch. While I was leaning over the roof of the cage, I scratched myself on a stick.'

The doctor turns over Bengt's right hand.

'There's a small scratch just above the right wrist. Six, seven millimetres and somewhat healed.'

Senior Constable Magnusson narrows his eyes.

'How long have you had that one then, Bengt?'

'I don't know. But I had it last Friday, because I tore the scab off in class.'

The doctor starts to take a blood sample. Bengt looks up at the ceiling while a needle is inserted into his arm.

At ten past five Constable Björk signals to Bengt that it's time to go.

'We're going to go look at a place,' he says.

Björk leads him out to a car. Senior Constable Magnusson sits in the front, while Mr Ekvall is already waiting in the back. Björk drives in the direction of the football field. But they go past it and head onto a country road. They park near the dump. Senior Constable Magnusson steps around the car and grimaces at the mud. Constable Björk turns to Bengt.

'Okay, Bengt. Can you show us exactly what you did on Friday?'

Bengt takes a small step, then heads up towards a ridge without any hesitation.

'Can you point to the place where you saw something red you believed was a cigarette stamp?'

He does so.

'And then what did you do with it, when you realised it wasn't what you were looking for?'

Bengt glances around, bewildered. Then he raises his arm and points.

'I threw it over there, I think.'

Constable Björk heads over to search. He finds nothing.

'And where did you get muddy, Bengt? You said you slipped?'

'Yes, I walked out on the bar there. And slipped off.'

Bengt heads over. When he reaches the point where the ground slopes down to the water's surface, he stops and points. Out in the water an old chicken coop lies half submerged. He had stepped on the slats of the side frame to reach the red paper, he explains.

'First I slipped with my left shoe. And then with my right.'

'Did you get your feet wet?'

'Yeah, near the heel. And a little in the sole.'

After a while they head back to the car.

'Now, Bengt, we're taking you to Ljungaskog.'

'What's that?'

'A state-run children's home, located near Örkelljunga.'

'What will I do there?'

All three men turn to face him. Mr Ekvall speaks the words.

'We at the Child Welfare Board have decided it's the best place for you.'

'Can't I go home?'

'No, you can't go home just yet.'

'Why?'

Mr Ekvall sighs and stuffs his hands in his pockets.

'At least half of Perstorp thinks you're a murderer, Bengt. It's not safe for you at home.'

Two weeks after Sam's birth, Justus, Sam and I all attended a wedding. It really was too early for something like that. But I was so eager for my life to return to normal. I thought normal was something I could get back, thought pregnancy was just a phase, and now it was over. I didn't know yet that pregnancies never end; they go on for a lifetime.

After the ceremony, we all ate sitting at long tables outside. Sam lay in the crook of my left arm, while I struggled to eat with my right. Periodically, people came over to look at the baby.

'He's so cute!' they'd say, and 'He looks just like you!' or 'He's a tiny copy of Justus!'

Fredrik also came over. With his hands behind his back, he bent over Sam and stared into his sightless eyes with his own big blue ones. He looked thoughtful. Then he straightened up.

'Well, I don't know what to say,' he said. 'It's a baby.'

I roared with laughter.

PSYCHOLOGISTS PUT IN CHARGE

The boy has been placed at the Ljungaskog Reformatory in Örkelljunga. Interrogators consider it pointless at present to seek any further admissions from a minor suspect using normal methods of interrogation. Instead, it will now be the task of professional psychologists to encourage the minor to talk, to clarify any factors in his past, heritage, environment, upbringing, etc., that may have contributed to the terrible act he's accused of. [. . .]

'As of early Wednesday, one of Sweden's most prominent child psychologists, Torsten Thysell of Karlstad, has travelled to Ljungaskog to take over the boy's care,' Advisor Stenkula tells a reporter from the newspaper *Dagens Nyheter.* 'What the boy needs most right now is peace and quiet. I've already spoken with him, but in no way referred to the murder. It's up to the authorities now to proceed with the utmost caution so as this boy's whole life doesn't end up destroyed.' [. . .]

On Tuesday the police were continuing with routine investigations in Perstorp, gathering witness statements, and combing the area surrounding the murder scene. They have found no new evidence to work with.

I laugh bitterly when I read that. Five days have passed since Birgitta was murdered. And already it's painfully clear that they've singled out Bengt as the perpetrator. *They have found no new evidence to work with.* I wish I could call these

153

investigators and ask them: what about the man Elin Sjöberg saw? What about all of the other men who were in the area? How about checking the make and size of all their shoes, not just the migrant factory workers'? Could it be possible there are more than just one pair of Tretorn-branded shoes in size 42 in Perstorp? Could it be that, just like in any small town, there's just *one* shoe store where everyone buys their shoes? Was that perhaps where Edvin Oskarsson bought the shoes, also from Tretorn, that he later gave to Bengt? I angrily slam my computer shut and throw my pen on the floor. The sound as it hits the rug is unsatisfactorily undramatic. I walk into the bathroom and meet my own hostile gaze before pressing my forehead against the cold mirror.

The Ljungaskog reformatory, now called a youth home, still exists. There's a thread from 2016 on the online forum Flashback entitled 'Warning: Ljungaskog institution's inhumane treatment of clients and staff!' If there were abuses going on in 2016, I can only imagine what 1948 was like. Most of what I can find out about the place is from recent years. There are official complaints filed regarding sexual abuse, verbal abuse, violence, suicide attempts and even one hostage situation. Trawling the archives of one of the main newspapers, I read every article published between 1948 and 1950 that mentions Ljungaskog. There are a striking number of escape attempts reported, but no one asks *why* these boys keep running away. Instead, the articles and notices are about locals fed up with these boys stealing bikes and cars, or breaking into summer cottages.

After an initial meeting with Bengt at Ljungaskog, Dr Thysell describes his impression of him to a reporter:

A delightful boy. He definitely doesn't seem to be the emotional type, so I find it difficult to connect him to the crime he's suspected of. But the investigation has just begun, and the human psyche contains many nooks, crannies and almost unfathomable depths.

In that same article, the mood in Perstorp is described as bitter. This bitterness *is particularly directed at football coach Edvin Oskarsson, who first raised suspicions by reporting that he had seen the boy heading into the forest. Some people are not hesitant to point to Oskarsson as the real culprit. However, his alibi is airtight, according to the police.* This alibi consists of the fact that Edvin was observed coming out of the changing room at the new football field sometime between half past seven and a quarter to eight. One person remembers Edvin exchanging a few words with a couple of other men, while another person saw him cycling away in the company of someone else. Edvin himself says he talked to a few people in the changing room, but never mentions anyone biking away with him. He says he rode to Assar Andersson's alone. There are no interviews with Andersson in the police investigation. But someone must have spoken to him, because there's a summary of a conversation that allegedly took place on 11 May included in the court documents. It's five lines long:

Hauler Assar Andersson, Mailbox 539, Perstorp: 49 years old

On May 7, 1948 at approximately 7:30pm, Edvin Oskarsson visited Andersson. He paid a bill for hauling services. Afterwards, they stood in the yard talking for at least 20 minutes. At 8:15pm, one of Andersson's farmhands arrived home.

By then Edvin was already gone.

Constable Björk is sitting at his dark wooden desk. His head rests heavily on his left hand. In his right, he holds a letter, and in front of him sits a huge pile of the same. All need to be read, even if they're just the fantasies of lunatics and neurotics.

The lad is innocent! I'm the murberer. I paved the girl.

murberrer

Constable Björk snorts. A warm summer evening beckons outside his window. Some well-meaning secretary has placed a vase of purple lilacs in the office. Their scent is almost over-powering. Sweat trickles down his skin, and the light of the desk lamp reflects off the constable's shiny face. When he gets home, he'll lie right down on his cool bed, on top of the blanket. His wife will cook dinner and open a cold beer for him. She'll call him when it's time to eat on the patio. He'll spend the late evening by the radio, listening to the midnight concert. He envisions it all while picking up the next letter from the pile. The paper is thick and a dusty pink. Someone's taped cut-out newspaper letters to it. They form three words:

Find
serviceman
Samuelsson.

'Oh well, thanks for the tip,' he mutters. The next letter-writer thinks that the police should scrutinise the football coach more closely. Then there's a Mrs Maria in Lund who had a strange dream and felt compelled to write two densely transcribed pages and send them to the police. A certain E.C. is also sure that coach Edvin Oskarsson is the culprit, as is the person who signs her letter as 'also a Mother', who wonders what Oskarsson was doing that required so much handwashing in the changing room. One astrologer is seeking out the precise time and date of Bengt's birthday. Constable Björk throws the letter aside and get up out of his seat. He wants someone to share this idiocy with. He heads out of his office in search of a colleague, only to realise he's now alone. Reluctantly, he heads back to his desk and sinks down heavily.

> Release the Perstorp boy, he's innocent. I have confessed it already,
> so do not pressure the Child. The war has turnt me to a murderer.
> Keep the lassies in at night. He couldn't lift that stone.
> The Killer

It's now half past six in the evening. Constable Björk strokes his right index finger back and forth across his upper lip while tapping his left foot against the floor. His stomach has started to ache with hunger. The next letter was given to them by Birgitta's father earlier today, one of the many addressed to him. 'Poor bastard,' the constable says aloud to himself. It's from a self-proclaimed clairvoyant. He wants Birgitta's father to send him a piece of Birgitta's clothing and signs the letter as 'Croo-Maat'. Most of the people that write to Valdemar Sivander are of that type – charlatans. One of them writes page after page about evil spirits released by the war.

> If the murderer was not yet dead when he committed the deed,
> no doubt he is with us physically alive and physically alive

157

*himself. If he lacked a physical body at the time of the crime,
it is most likely that he later possessed the body of the boy.
You, the parents and relatives, might be able to solve this case
if you turn to the clairvoyants for help. But You must believe
in the Seer, otherwise you will deprive him of his power.
Afterwards, you can review the material you received, preferably
with the help of an older man born in October.*

Another asks for their letter to be forwarded to Bengt's father.
It was revealed to them in a dream that the boy is innocent.
A third letter-writer inherited a so-called 'dancing table', a
device supposedly able to communicate with spirits, and despite
not believing in such junk himself, the writer asked the table
a series of questions. The table apparently conveyed the killer's
name was Hugo Eriksson, a farmer who likes to play sports.
He's 34 years old, unmarried and lives in Perstorp.

Constable Björk feels a heaviness in his chest. People are
not smart. He had no idea there were so many lunatics in this
country. Beneath that letter is one signed 'Friend of Truth';
this one also suspects Edvin Oskarsson. The constable decides
to collect all the letters that point to Oskarsson in a special
pile. He counts 26 before he finally turns off the light and
locks the door of the police station. In one, a civil engineer
reports he's heard rumours that Oskarsson is a Nazi.

I'm surprised there are so many like this. Do the police still
receive letters about people's dreams when there's a high-
profile murder case? It's difficult for me to take these letters
seriously. Perhaps I should be more sceptical when interpreting
my own dreams and horoscopes.

It's Friday 21 May 1948. Birgitta's been dead for two weeks, and Bengt's been moved three times. At the moment he's in a psychiatric clinic in Lund. Dr Thysell has followed him there and they've spoken many times. When Bengt screams that he can't take more interrogations, throwing his arms over his head in despair, the doctor calmly repeats that this is not an interrogation, but an analysis. Bengt understands that the doctor is here to assess his state of mind. But while the doctor assesses Bengt, Bengt is also assessing him, trying to figure out what's going on inside the doctor's head. Does he believe Bengt is guilty?

Bengt goes to lie down on an iron bed. The rubber under-sheet squeaks uncomfortably. He misses the bed he shared with his little brother. He yearns for nothing more than to sit at the top of the stairs talking to Axel. What if Mama, Papa, Siv and Axel believe he's a murderer? Nothing will ever be the same again. At night he dreams of the policemen's eyes. They stare and their gazes bore into his head.

When Bengt is awoken on Saturday morning, he feels like he hasn't slept a wink. The nurse looks unsure. Her eyes flicker like a flame.

A male attendant comes in and makes his bed, and then a doctor arrives.

'It's time to talk to the police again, Bengt.'

Bengt chews his breakfast extremely slowly. The doctor stands there for a bit, staring at him, with his journal pad balanced on folded arms in front of his stomach.

'Yes, take your time to eat,' he says. 'The interrogation won't start until after lunch.'

When Bengt opened up the bag that Mama and Papa packed for him, he found a book inside. *The Call of the Wild*. He's already read it three times, but he opens the cover to start for a fourth time. The shouts and chatter of patients and their attendants grow ever more distant. The whole morning has passed by the time Bengt reads the last paragraph. He reads it twice more before closing the book and pulling the blanket over his head. Bengt closes his eyes and imagines wide vistas wolves, and a vast deserted night sky. He dreams so intensely of the wilderness that he's almost surprised he's not there when the attendant comes to collect him.

It's the last day of the semester at Central school in Perstorp. The classrooms are decorated with birch branches. Wreaths have been drawn on the blackboard in chalk. In the middle stands this happy message: *Summer vacation starts now!* Parents and younger siblings are lined up along the walls, watching with gentle eyes while the teachers display what they've taught their students during the term. Like well-trained dogs, the students stretch their small arms towards the ceiling. Margit smiles and nods, but Valdemar finds it all unbearable. Enormous effort has been made to keep the Sivander family and the Sommer family out of sight of each other today. After the children are given lilacs by their teachers, Valdemar and Margit take Karl home in their car. The suitcases are already packed. They're leaving as soon as they've eaten. In the schoolyard, the celebration of the end of the school year continues. The girls in Birgitta's class are dressed as flowers. They sport bluebells, roses, apple blossom and violets made of crepe paper. The children sing so purely that every mother has tears in her eyes.

At home, the Sivander family eat herring and potatoes in silence. Valdemar opens another beer. The clock is ticking on the wall, and somewhere outside the open window, beyond the garden, someone shouts, 'Hurray! Hurray! Hurray! Hurray!'

'Enough,' Margit says, standing up to collect the plates. 'We're surely done now.'

They load their suitcases into the trunk, then set off for the wide beaches of Haverdal, two hours to the north. On their

161

way, they pick up a girl. Maria is the daughter of the widow who cleans for the Sivander family, a year younger than Karl. She's going to help take care of Eva. They see it as a good deed, taking the daughter of a hard-working widow out to the country for some sun and fresh air. No one considers that perhaps the widow is the one performing the good deed, allowing the Sivander family to borrow her daughter when they lack one of their own. When Maria's curls bounce in the corner of your eye, you might even be able to pretend for a moment that they're Birgitta's.

'You need to go get a haircut, Karl, as soon as we arrive.'

Margit turns her face towards the back seat as she speaks. She's wearing black sunglasses, concealing her eyes. Margit hasn't really looked directly at her children since 7 May. Karl stares at her profile and feels a sudden longing to lay his head at the point where her neck meets her shoulder. He nods and stares out the window. Stone houses and factories whizz by, soon to be replaced by old farms and wide fields.

As they get closer, Valdemar opens the window and the strong, clean scent of saltwater and seaweed fills the car. They pull it into their lungs and let the dry, oppressive air of anxiety flow out with the wind. Valdemar turns in towards a bright house just above the rugged beach. Tall yew trees are standing like a ring of guards around the house. On the back side there's a line of ancient, windblown winter oaks. When they climb out of the car, Valdemar puts an arm around Margit's waist. Karl hasn't seen him do that in a long time. His parents stand facing the sparkling sea. Maria takes Eva in her arms and heads into the house with Erik.

Karl watches his parents' backs for a little before going inside. There are colourful rag rugs on the floors. He and Erik will share a bed in one of the small, old-fashioned bedrooms. Karl doesn't protest. It feels safe to have his brother close.

After unpacking, they're set free. Karl and Erik run over the chalky white dunes, tear off their clothes and throw themselves into the waves. The water is ice cold. Erik immediately wants to get out again, but Karl persuades him to stay.

'If you dip your head just once, it'll feel warm.'

Erik looks at Karl sceptically as he dunks his head under. A thousand salty streams flow down his brother's face. Erik follows suit.

'You were right,' he says after a while.

Karl and Erik drift in silence next to each other. From the house, they look like small black dots against the sun.

After they've finished swimming, they sit on the stones that form the border between the beach and the grass. Their bodies slowly dry and begin warming in the sun. Erik fingers a plant with clusters of very small purple flowers.

'What's this called?'

'I don't know,' Karl says.

Erik grabs a bunch of another plant and rubs it between his fingers. He smells it.

'What is this then? It smells like a spice.'

Karl rises from his half-lying position and smells the plant in his little brother's hand.

'I don't know, Erik.'

'Birgitta would have known,' says Erik quietly.

'You're probably right.'

Further down the beach, Maria is walking slowly with her hands on her back. She's watching Eva, who's sitting among sandy stones. Maria's sundress billows in the wind. The brothers squint at her until their mother's voice becomes faintly audible over the wind and waves.

'Time to get a haircut, Karl,' she says when they get upstairs. 'I'll take you.'

It's a long walk to the centre of town. His mother points to the barber's sign and presses a few coins into Karl's hand.

'I have to do some shopping. Stay inside when you're done, and I'll pick you up.'

Karl steps in. Both of the barber's chairs are occupied, so he sits and wait his turn.

'Yep . . .' One of the customers carries on his conversation with the first barber. 'There are just so many terrible things happening.'

Karl's beckoned to the chair.

'I still have a hard time imagining it could be him,' says the other barber.

'I have to agree with you on that. I just can't imagine . . .'

The barber behind Karl's back measures the length of his hair and picks up his scissors.

'. . . that a young boy could do something like that,' he continues.

Karl freezes. The barber starts cutting, quickly and efficiently, while talking.

'A boy of 14. And he looked skinny in the picture, too.'

'But they say he's strong,' the customer in the other chair interjects.

'Sure, but to have the balls to do such a thing . . .'

The barber glances at Karl in the mirror. Karl looks past him, staring into nothingness.

'How old are you?'

'I'm 12,' Karl replies in a more childish voice than he'd intended.

'Do you believe a boy only two years older than you could kill a 9-year-old girl in cold blood? And then bury her under a bunch of rocks and moss.'

'I don't know.'

Karl sits in silence while the men continue to discuss the murder of his little sister. When he's done, he pays quickly and heads out into the street. It takes his mother forever to show up. The sun beats down relentlessly onto his skin. When she finally arrives, she angrily grabs him by the arm.

'You were supposed to wait inside!'

That evening, Karl and Erik are lying in bed, foot to head, staring up at the ceiling. They can hear their parents talking quietly to each other through the open window.

Karl hears a sob from Erik's end of the bed and sits up. He moves his pillow and lies down next to Erik and wraps an arm around him. After a few minutes the tears subside, and his brother's breathing deepens.

Unrelentingly grey clouds hang low over Stockholm, reflected in the many windows of the police station on a spring day in 1948. Gusts of cold wind blow as Monday's mail arrives. A number of packages are addressed to the National Forensic Science Institute. They contain items with fingerprints on them, soiled clothing, guns and bloody hammers from all over the country. One by one, the packages are distributed onto desks. The largest and heaviest is placed on Detective Otto Sahlén's table. It's from Perstorp. Detective Sahlén has heard about the murder of the young girl, and about the 14-year-old suspect. It's in the papers every day. The package contains the boy's shoes, three plaster casts from the ditch Birgitta was found in, and a large jar of soil from the crime scene.

'They've gathered too much dirt again, idiots,' Detective Sahlén mutters to his colleague Stellan. 'The geologists aren't going to be happy.'

He places the jar on the desk with a heavy thump.

Sahlén can already see that Bengt's shoes match the plaster casts. There's the same pattern on the soles – squares composed of slanted lines, turned alternately from right to left. The logo from the brand Tretorn is also visible. The shoes being compared to the prints are made of fabric with a rubber heel and sole. The factory informed them the model is described as a 'grey heeled shoe, article number 150' in their catalogue, and that they were manufactured in January of 1948. The shoes are well worn and stained. Detective Sahlén scrapes dirt from

166

them into a paper bag. This will be sent to the geologists and compared to a sample from the crime scene.

Sahlén and Stellan then try to determine if the prints in the ditch could have been made by Bengt's shoes. The clearest cast is from a left-footed shoe, so they start with that one. They pour a bit of the soil sample into a container with a springy bottom. Using Bengt's shoes, they make impressions in it, and compare these with the casts from the ditch. They push the shoes down into containers of soil from other places too, to see if it makes any difference. It's soon clear that shoes of the same model and size did leave a footprint at the murder scene. But whether they were actually Bengt's shoes, the detective and Stellan cannot say for certain.

In one square on Bengt's soles, the lines in the pattern taper slightly. This could have been caused by an air bubble forming between the rubber and the mould, they tell him at the Tretorn factory when Detective Sahlén calls. A random defect. But it could also be the result of wear and tear, which would mean it's not necessarily unique to Bengt's shoes. He heads upstairs and asks an engineer to try to determine if the same defect can be seen in the casts from the crime scene. There is something there, but it's not clear. Sahlén notes a few small, dark spots on the shoes. They might be blood.

'Let the lab take a look at them,' he says to Stellan, handing over the shoes, 'and then send them to Lundkvist along with that cask of soil. I'm sure he'll love that!'

The detective's boisterous laughter follows his colleague out into the corridor. As Stellan reaches the stairs, his deferential smile disappears. He hopes he doesn't end up taking the blame for the outsized soil sample.

The letter that arrives a week later from the state geologist Gösta Lundkvist at the Geological Survey of Sweden reports what he found after carefully boiling the samples and examining them under a microscope. It reads like poetry, the essence of a forest in text form: mire, chips of birch bark, peat and mineral grains. Pollen from birch, and a few from alder, oak, elm, spruce, pine and hazel. Moss, heather and a bit of green algae.

A complete pollen analysis of this sample was not considered necessary, since it was not adequately collected. It should have been taken from the surface layer and just below and no thicker than a couple of cm3. This same mistake seems to be made consistently, by the way, when samples are collected by non-experts.

The state geologist concludes that Bengt's shoes were in a place similar to the site of the murder – a wet bog in a birch grove. But, he adds, there are many such places.

Dr Thysell shuffles his papers, reading a little, humming to himself before the meeting begins. He's in the lecture hall of the psychiatric clinic in Lund. Seated around an oval table are 15 serious men and women. The sun reflects off the shiny surface of the table, and one young woman is ordered to draw the curtains. Everyone at this gathering is dressed in shades of brown. They chat quietly while coffee is served. A burst of laughter escapes one of the younger men, and Thysell winces. He stares pointedly at the man.

The meeting begins with a count of those present, while the graduate student Schunnesson takes minutes. Thysell is acquainted with her father. Schunnesson's pen scratches quickly across the paper. The case is first summarised by Circuit Judge Davidsson, and the floor is then given over to Senior Constable Magnusson. Three boys in Bengt's class were asked to describe Bengt as a classmate, and they all agreed that he was the strongest boy in their class, but not naughty. One boy, who weighs a bit less and seems weaker than Bengt, was asked to lift the heaviest of the stones placed atop Birgitta's dead body. He did so without difficulty. The same boy was made to re-enact Bengt's supposed actions at the dump, and he didn't get any mud on his shoes. Bengt's and Birgitta's clothes have been sent to the National Forensic Science Institute, but no response has yet been received.

After reviewing the case and the investigative work done so far, it's time to call in Bengt for questioning. Seven jurors leave the room. They're all natives of Perstorp, and they think that might make Bengt less likely to tell the truth.

Bengt's freckles have faded, and he seems dull and listless. Senior Constable Magnusson begins by stating that the examination of Bengt's clothes is complete, and that bloodstains were found on them. The eight adults around the table look at Bengt. Magnusson demands an answer. *Why* was there blood on his clothes? He asks if Bengt had any nosebleeds, or if he's been involved in the butchering of chickens or rabbits. Bengt says no. His eyes seem to rove around the room. Finally, he seems to find what he's looking for.

'When the doctor took the blood sample, there was some blood on the tip of the syringe. Maybe it dripped onto my pants, maybe that's how it got there,' says Bengt hopefully.

Senior Constable Magnusson observes him silently.

'You surely know you're a suspect, Bengt,' he says finally, and Bengt lowers his eyes. The senior constable begins counting on his fingers, while his voice gets louder and louder. 'To begin with, you told us you hadn't been up in the forest. Only after Oskarsson reported seeing you did you admit that you went to the dump. You tried to wash away the bloodstains. You lied on occasions before that as well.' He narrows his eyes angrily at Bengt. 'Please stick to the truth now.'

Dr Thysell raises a reassuring hand and takes over the questioning. Quietly, he asks Bengt if he saw anyone in the forest. Bengt shakes his head.

'Are you afraid of someone?' he continues.

'No,' Bengt murmurs.

'Why didn't you go with the other boys to the ditch where they found Birgitta?' continues Dr Thysell. 'Weren't you curious? Boys usually are.'

'A lot of boys didn't go there.'

Thysell takes a deep breath. Then he takes out a picture of Birgitta. Her vivid black and white eyes are reflected in Bengt's pupils.

'Have you thought much about Birgitta?' says Dr Thysell.

'No,' Bengt says, looking from the picture to the doctor.

The doctor holds the picture up for a few more seconds, before putting it down.

'Why wouldn't you like it if a photograph of you appeared in the papers?'

Bengt slouches against the back of his chair and stares downwards. That was a question that he'd asked one of the nurses, in confidence.

'I just asked if there was a photo of me in there.'

'Yes, a newspaper did publish a picture of you. But that's been dealt with firmly. It won't happen again.' Thysell is silent for a few seconds. 'Do you want to go home?'

The moment the doctor asks the question, Bengt bursts into tears. The adults sit in silence while his shoulders shake and tears stream down his face.

'Do you think that you were treated as you deserved, or do you think that you should have been treated differently?' Dr Thysell asks mildly.

'You should have let me stay at home,' says Bengt.

Bengt is sent back to his iron bed, and after a short break 15 people are seated in the lecture hall again. Senior Constable Magnusson is reading some papers when the circuit judge knocks hard on the table in front of him. Magnusson looks up with an expression of childish fright.

'Senior Constable, would you be so kind as to present the results you've received?'

Magnusson stubs out his cigarette.

'Yes, the reports from the State Forensic Institute. As I mentioned earlier, bloodstains were found on Bengt's clothes. To summarise, the stains on the shoes are best described as insignificant, but are also most likely human blood. How long they've been there and the blood type could not be determined. And then there's the larger stain on the right arm of the jacket . . .' Magnusson flips back through his papers. '. . . which was approximately one by four centimetres. Probably type A blood. Which, unfortunately, doesn't get us anywhere, because both Birgitta and Bengt have type A1. Professor Sjöwall investigated the blood according the MNS system as well, and determined that Birgitta had MN and Bengt, N. Unfortunately, Bengt's shirt and jacket were sent in a thermos that broke in transport, and arrived soaked in saline. Because of that, the lab was unable to determine if the spots were made by MN or N blood.'

A frustrated silence spreads through the room. A balding man wearing thick black glasses and a grim expression raises his hand.

'Yes, Dr Essen-Möller?' says the circuit judge.

'Professor Sjöwall believed that at least the larger of the spots looked like it had been washed. Did forensics agree with that?'

'They couldn't determine if any of the stains had been washed,' Senior Constable Magnusson replies. 'But the stains on the inside of the shirt sleeves were probably old.'

A woman in her fifties raises an index finger. It's Ingrid Ydström from Perstorp's Child Welfare Board. The circuit judge raises his eyebrows and nods.

'Yes, Mrs Ydström?'

'Bengt had a scratch here,' she says, pointing to her own left wrist. 'Of about four centimetres?'

'Yes, that's correct,' replies the circuit judge.

'Wouldn't it be reasonable to suppose the stain came from the incident Bengt himself reported, when he cut himself on the rabbit hutch he was helping a friend build?'

No one answers. The Child Welfare Board are the ones who will ultimately decide if Bengt should be allowed to return to his parents or be placed in a juvenile institution. It's seldom anyone from the board brings up anything to indicate his possible innocence. Why don't they? Why do they so badly want Bengt to be guilty? If it were me sitting there, surely I would have done everything I could to point out facts that spoke against one child murdering another?

The circuit judge turns to the doctor.

'Well, Dr Thysell, you've met Bengt a number of times now. What did you find out?'

Thysell clears his throat.

'Well, I cannot say that I've come to any strong conclusions yet as to whether or not Bengt committed the crime.'

'How does he react when you bring up Birgitta in your conversations?'

Thysell folds his hands in his lap, glances up at the ceiling and takes his time before answering.

'Emotionally cool and cautious,' he says briefly and meets the circuit judge's eyes. 'However, I want to emphasise one thing,' he continues after a few seconds of silence, 'and that concerns Bengt changing his story. It doesn't necessarily mean anything for a boy his age. On the contrary, I would find it strange if he didn't.'

'Yes,' mutters the circuit judge, pointing indolently at Bengt's lawyer, Bertil Peyron, who has indicated that he'd like to speak.

Peyron adjusts the lapels of his jacket.

'There's no doubt there are some troubling circumstances surrounding Bengt. But if you examine the evidence more closely, you'll see there's no proof here that he had anything to do with the murder.'

He picks up his papers and flips to the page with pictures of Bengt's clothes. With no body inside, they look abandoned.

'First of all, these clothes may have been washed and restained many times over. And secondly, there's nothing odd about an active 14-year-old boy having stains on his clothing that he can't explain. When I made my way to the football field as Bengt had, I passed two barbed wire fences and scratched an ankle, which bled through my sock.'

'And what, Mr Peyron, do you have to say about Bengt changing his story, first claiming he went straight home then finally admitting he was up in the woods?'

Senior Constable Magnusson is speaking now. He has assumed the same sulking position as Thysell – leaning far back and with his arms crossed. Peyron counters by leaning even further forward. He narrows his hazel eyes at the constable.

'He has already explained that he was afraid of being associated with the murder. Please remember he is only 14 years old.'

It must have occurred to someone in that group that one person at the football field that evening had been able make Bengt change his story – Edvin Oskarsson. It was only after

Oskarsson reported to the police that he saw Bengt walking towards the forest, and after the football coach's tête-à-tête with him, that the boy had admitted taking a detour on the way home. But nobody says so. Peyron allows the silence to linger before continuing.

'Don't you think it seems rather unlikely that a 14-year-old would have committed such a brutal crime? That he would even be physically capable of doing it?'

'His classmate was able to lift the stone without a problem,' objects Magnusson.

'Yes, but many stones had to be lifted. And dug out of the earth.'

Violent red spots have appeared on Senior Constable Magnusson's cheeks. He opens his mouth, but doesn't have time to say more before Peyron continues.

'In my opinion, the evidence points to a lunatic. Not a normal 14-year-old. A boy who seemed completely normal when he met his neighbour on the way home. Not even short of breath.'

Peyron lets that land before continuing. Magnusson's face looks like he just lost a race because his opponent cheated.

'Condemning him to a juvenile correction facility would be the same as sentencing him for the murder. I hope you all understand that. And it's not something that should be done simply on mere suspicion. I spoke to Bengt's mother today, and she agrees that he shouldn't return home to Perstorp at this time, for his own safety. There are large crowds outside their home, reporters chasing them down, and Bengt may well be attacked by someone who believes he's guilty.'

'Not to mention how unpleasant it would be for the Sivander family. We can't subject their son to attending school with the person who *probably murdered his sister*,' says Magnusson. He receives a warning finger from the circuit judge.

Mr Peyron stares at the constable in outrage before continuing.

175

'Mrs Sommer has a brother in Halmstad who can take care of the boy for a while.'

Peyron lights another cigarette before confidentially leaning forward and meeting the eyes of each and every person.

'It's like this. Bengt may know more than he's telling us. He may well have seen something.' He pauses for effect before continuing. 'I think he might have been intimidated into silence.'

Something wakes me up. It is an early summer morning and Justus is already up with Sam, still a baby. I hear a sound I don't recognise, a long howl. Like a wounded animal. A dog? Dressed in nothing but my underpants, I open the bedroom door. The sound gets louder. Everything inside me freezes. I walk with my eyes closed across the stone floor of the hall and around the corner to the living room. When I open my eyes, I see Justus sitting on the sofa. The sound is coming from his open mouth. His eyes are closed and Sam is in his arms. Justus's left arm is limp, his phone in his palm. I stand completely still for a long moment, as that inhuman sound pours out of his throat. Finally, he opens his eyes.

'Fredrik's dead,' he screams, 'Fredrik's dead.'

Bengt's trial – which was not technically a trial, but for lack of a better word is still called that – is approaching. The Child Welfare Board's representative, the lawyer Einar Bjure-Dahlén, sits in his office in Stockholm, reading the forensic reports. He's under a great deal of strain and he's not happy. Bengt had blood on his clothes, but in tiny amounts and the stains might have been old. Someone with shoes of the same model and size as Bengt did walk in that ditch, but there's no evidence they were Bengt's in particular. Bjure-Dahlén angrily throws the papers away from him, they slide across the table and fall to the floor. Muttering to himself, he stands and gathers them up again, places them in the correct order and shoves a paper clip around them.

'Pettersson!' he shouts out into the corridor.

A young intern looks in.

'Pettersson, could you please send this to the Danes,' he says and hands the young man the investigations.

'Of course. For a second opinion?' he asks.

'*Yes*, for a second opinion,' Bjure-Dahlén snarls, but immediately seems to regret his harshness. He continues more quietly, almost whispering. 'What would it look like if we allowed a murderer to walk the streets because of our carelessness.' He sighs. 'We might end up with a *crime wave* of little girls being murdered in this country. The Danes are considered the best at this kind of thing. If anyone can determine whether or not those were Bengt's footprints, it's them.'

There are so many young men buried at Skogskyrkogården cemetery. There are even pictures of some – images engraved onto headstones or photos taped to stone, their corners curled from condensation. I stop and look at those pictures. Sons and brothers. Why did they have to die so young? In their photos they seem fearless, while high up in my big apartment I am filled with terror that something might happen to one of *my* children.

Suicide is the most common cause of death for young men, followed by accidents and drug overdoses. Some have died violent deaths, in shootings. Of course, they might also have died like Fredrik: a brain haemorrhage, rapid and unforeseeable. I wonder if the ones who pass so quickly can find their way after death. It happened so suddenly, Justus can't seem to accept that Fredrik is gone. Is it the same for the dead?

Violence entered Sam's life when he was 3. That's when the children in his preschool started to divide up into boys and girls. The girls got quieter. They worked on crafts or pretended to be cats. The boys started hitting. There were some older boys that Sam wanted to be friends with. Every day after preschool he told me they wanted to fight, and he didn't think it was fun. But he wanted to be around them, which meant having to take it, having to get hit sometimes. When Sam changed preschools, we thought things would get better. And they did, but violence didn't go away completely. It's something he's just expected to accept. Maybe he's hit someone too, some other boy who went home to be consoled?

179

I don't think so, but what do I know about the world of little boys?

I do my best to instil empathy and kindness in him, but I don't know if I truly have that power. Sometimes it feels the Turtles, the Avengers and the Karl XII documentary he watches on repeat are raising him, not me. It doesn't matter if I tell him no toy guns, because now he has two swords and a shield, and has built guns out of Lego. If he doesn't have access to any of these, his soft hands can always turn a stick into a weapon. I lost control of the situation a long time ago.

The day before Bengt's trial is set to begin, Einar Bjure-Dahlén receives a letter from the Danish police's technical department in Copenhagen. The Danish technicians agree with their Swedish colleagues: the shoe prints at the scene of the murder are of the same size and make as Bengt's. Furthermore, they've studied the manufacturing error or the pattern of wear on Bengt's left sole and compared it to the footprints. They think there may be a corresponding deviation in the squares. They did not find the same detail when they compared impressions from the soles of a pair of new Tretorn shoes.

They conclude with the following: *There is a high probability that the accused's left shoe could have made the cast footprint.*

Pictures of the soles and castings are attached. The casts are rough, rugged and full of holes, especially on the side where the unevenness of Bengt's soles is found.

At Klippan's courthouse there's an almost carnival-like atmosphere the next morning. The line to get inside seems to wind endlessly. On this first day the curtains will be pulled open, and everyone wants to see the show. *Dagens Nyheter* refers to the murder as 'The Mysterious May Drama' – which sounds like the title of a detective novel.

The trial begins at ten, and not until half past six that evening will the audience's hundreds of shoes scrape against the floor as they emerge hungry and tired into a summer evening. How many of them will experience nightmares that night? I know I did after reading the records, and I didn't have to watch as the pointed rock found beneath Birgitta's head was dropped onto the table in the courtroom with a thud.

The next day *Dagens Nyheter* writes:

The so-called key witness, coach Edvin Oskarsson, did not make a strong impression in court. He had difficulty understanding the interrogator's questions, and his answers didn't always indicate a clear understanding of the subject matter.

Edvin seems reluctant to mention Bengt by name in court and usually refers to him simply as 'the boy'. In recounting his observations, he says he saw 'a lady' in the company of some children on the road, but he can't say for sure who she was or how many were present. He previously told the police that it was the Bloms' nanny, Sonja, accompanied by Birgitta. Also contradicting his initial statement to the police, he denies that he asked Bengt if he'd gone into the forest, after his visit to the crime scene with the young football players. 'That is completely unfamiliar to me,' he adds in the trial.

I know witnesses are unreliable. Testimonies can change. I understand that Edvin can't remember exactly how he expressed himself on that first Saturday. But if he previously remembered seeing the murdered girl with Sonja on that fateful Friday evening, then it feels like that story should remain somewhat consistent, doesn't it? Or was he never sure of what he'd seen?

The chairman follows up by asking how Bengt acted on the day after the murder, and Edvin answers:

I don't think I should answer such a question. On a day like that Saturday, I have to say, everyone in Perstorp was grieving, and you might get the wrong impression of a person on a day like that. I'm no "psychologist".

When the chairman asks what Edvin meant when he told the police Bengt's laugh didn't sound like it normally did, Edvin replies that he didn't really think about that before he said it. Did he feel guilty about dragging Bengt into this?

At the end of the interrogation, the chairman asks a few questions about Edvin's current state. Apparently, he quit as coach after the incident, and has temporarily moved home to his parents in another town. People have been cruel, and many newspapers pointed to him as a potential suspect. Edvin says he was afraid of having a mental breakdown.

By the time the interrogation ends, no one has asked him why, or when, he gave a pair of shoes to Bengt – the white canvas shoes that Rut mentioned and that Bengt chose not to wear on the night Birgitta was murdered. Edvin receives not a single question about shoes. I understand why: this trial is about determining if Bengt is guilty of Birgitta's murder, not Edvin. Edvin can't be treated like a suspect. But I'm left with a number of questions. Edvin told the police that his shoe size is 43, but he can fit in a 42. He also says that he hasn't worn canvas shoes for over ten years. But he does own a pair of gym shoes – white with rubber soles. What exactly is the difference between canvas shoes and gym shoes? The ones Bengt got from him were broken in, even more worn down than the ones Bengt had on the night of the murder. Could this mean that Edvin himself had worn them before?

When I first started to research Birgitta's case, I remember thinking Bengt was either innocent or a full-blown psychopath. How else to explain that he behaved normally after the murder? And how could he have withstood so many intense interrogations without confessing?

I think a lot about this case's *why*. I feel pretty sure that Birgitta's murder was unpremeditated. The killer didn't have a weapon with him. Instead, he reached for what was at hand, most likely a rock. It's never been found. Maybe he hid it somewhere? Perhaps he buried it along with his clothes, if the culprit was the man Elin Sjöberg saw at the edge of the forest? I discuss all this with Justus in the evenings, and he listens and comments.

'Who do *you* think it was?' he asks.

It occurs to me that he's never asked me this precise question before. I squeeze my lips together.

'Edvin, maybe,' I say after a while. 'Though there's nothing to really indicate it was him. It wouldn't hold up in court, of course. But . . .' I turn to Justus and start counting reasons on my fingers. 'He's the one who throws suspicion onto Bengt. He washes his hands but can't explain why. A reporter went to the same changing room and stood at the very same window and wrote that Edvin could not possibly have seen what he claimed to. Initially he tells the police he saw Birgitta, "whom he knew by sight", but in court he says that he didn't recognise the children he saw.'

I shrug.

'Those are some of the reasons. But it's more of a feeling. Honestly, I have no fucking clue. I believe something different almost every day.'

Justus stares into the distance and shakes his head.

'It's really weird,' he says.

I'm relieved that he's caught up in Birgitta's case too. Before I head off to brush my teeth, I turn back to him. He asks what it is.

'I don't know,' I say. 'It just gives me the creeps.'

'It would be strange if it didn't.'

He's right about that. But he doesn't understand what I'm truly saying – I'm asking for help. This murder is eating me alive. I'm not doing well. But I don't have it in me to make that clear to him. Besides, he can't help me. I'm too far gone.

I fall asleep in Vivi's bed while putting her down. When I wake up in the morning, the bed is empty. I can hear Vivi babbling from downstairs, while Justus reads a book to Sam. I'm dead tired, but I won't be able to fall back asleep. So I lay on my side and scroll through my phone. Then it happens again. Someone sits down on the bed behind me. I freeze and try to focus. The air vibrates. The mattress is sinking under someone's weight. I defiantly and obsessively look at Instagram post after Instagram post.

After a while the weight fades away. When the alarm goes off, I brace my body in a defensive posture. Then I throw off the covers, rush out of the room and slam the door behind me.

It's New Year's Day and my birthday. I'm turning 35. When I wake up, I can hear my family rummaging around downstairs. I sneak to the bathroom, doing my best to hide that I'm up. I've always found it overwhelming to be with other people all the time. When I was a kid I read constantly, and I accepted my own need for solitude completely.

When I reached my teens, I started to realise I was different, and forced myself to spend all my time with friends. I was just starting to accept my introverted nature again when I had children. It's not something you can indulge as a parent; I'm almost never alone. You give birth to a guilty conscience along with your child, a shadow copy of them that hangs by a rope from your heart, questioning everything you are and do as a parent. Justus gets up with the kids every morning, and often by the time I wake up, Vivi's spent hours without me. I think about how she might have been missing me while I was sleeping upstairs without a thought. The shadow child pulls on its rope.

The day doesn't go according to plan. I scold Sam for dragging Vivi around like a doll. He wants first this, then that. Lemon water and mandarin oranges. I'm caught between the children like a hunted antelope. I do my best to escape from Sam, who makes demand after demand after demand. I want to be alone. I need calm. My panic rises. Vivi cries and nothing I do works; every attempt is thwarted by Sam claiming my attention. I'm falling apart.

I skip putting on Vivi's pyjamas or brushing her teeth and head straight to her room to put her to bed. The second she's laid down, she flips over and starts crawling away. I put her down again and again. She rolls around, crawls away, wants free. It never seems to end. I'm reaching the point where you stop talking to your child like a child and start trying to reason with them like an adult. Pretend you can make them understand. After an hour, I turn on the light and pick her up. That's what she wants obviously. As we head down to Justus and Sam in the living room, she peers around curiously with red-rimmed eyes and wet cheeks. Sam wants me to look at what he's built in *Minecraft* and asks if he can have another mandarin. I can't take any more. I turn away. Sink into the armchair with a blank look on my face and Vivi in my arms.

I rally and make an effort to be a sweet, friendly, kind and calm mother. After gathering my strength for a little while I go back upstairs and gently put her down, over and over again. As she struggles to get up and crawl away the tears stream down her face. I sing and sing. Then I try not singing. I turn on the light and turn it off. When it's almost eight o'clock, I go back down with her again. By this time, I'm crying too. I put Vivi on the floor, and she crawls away.

'I can't do it anymore,' I whisper to Justus so Sam can't hear what a bad mother I am.

'It'll be okay. She will fall asleep eventually.'

I'm sobbing now.

Sam comes over and settles on my lap.

'Are you sad, Mummy?'

He stares up at me seriously. Justus goes out into the hall and comes back with Vivi, who's mad as a hornet now.

'I'm going to the bathroom, and after that you have to brush your teeth,' I tell Sam.

'But I don't wanna . . .' he starts.

I raise my hand to stop him. Stare hard at him. And then I head to the bathroom without another word. I steal a few seconds to scream silent profanities and throw imaginary plates at the locked door. Then I take a deep breath and hold it until I find the spot where my anxiety resides in my body and release it with my breath. I learned that from the yoga I studied during my worst time. I do it over again, holding my breath until I find that sharp, angular stone wedged into my sternum, and vomit it out. By the third time, my body feels softer, more compliant.

When I step out, I catch sight of myself in the hall mirror. Half of my hair is held up by an ugly clip to keep Vivi from pulling it, while the other half hangs in listless strands. I look like the Wicked Witch. When I pick Sam up, he protests, just like I knew he would. My eyes burn and my voice is aggressively quiet. He gives in to my will and lets me brush his teeth, while slumped over with eyes downcast. I can hear Vivi screaming through the closed door. Sam shows me his displeasure by turning his head to the side and not opening wide. I grab his chin. Not hard, but still, I'm angry. I know I'm making him sad, know it's unfair, but I can't stop myself from doing it. I feel like a trapped bear. I want to run far away. Out into the wilderness, alone.

I try to focus on feeling gratitude that my children are alive and well. I try to imagine how it would feel if I lost them, how much I'd yearn for an evening like this again. How I would trade anything for a toothbrush fight and night-nights that never end. It's a trick that usually works, but not now. Instead, I think the forbidden thought: I wish I didn't have any children.

'Should we have another kid?'

Justus's tone didn't reflect the enormity of the words he just said. They were so incongruous that I couldn't make sense of them the first time. I just stared. This was in the autumn of 2018, while the rain beat against the window of our second-floor apartment. I tried to sense if he was serious, or if he was just saying what he thought I wanted to hear. Loud squeals floated out of Sam's room, followed by the sound of toys spilling onto the floor. Sam and his friend had overturned a large basket of toys. Justus didn't look away from me. He smiled. I smiled.

And so Vivi's life began. I was so scared, but I wanted her. He wanted her too, but I didn't know that for sure until she arrived. When his eyes filled with tears. Then I understood we'd passed from the darkness into light. Like when the war ends, and the streamers and confetti are falling onto thousands of cheering people.

It was over, we had survived.

It's Wednesday 7 July 1948, the second day of the trial. The chairman is sitting at the front, like a king on his throne. The people on either side of him are lined up like Jesus's disciples. The Child Welfare Board members Ingrid Ydström and Sven Ekvall are in the audience. After her comment in the meeting at the psychiatric hospital in Lund, about the wound on Bengt's left arm corresponding to one of the bloodstains on his clothes, I've considered Ydström a kindred spirit, one of the few adults who might be on Bengt's side.

But my view of her has changed since I read the minutes from another meeting that reveal that on one occasion she, together with Ekvall and one other member of the board, picked up Bengt, herded him to the murder scene and tried to make him confess, all on her own initiative. I wonder what Ydström's and Ekvall's thoughts are in the courtroom, what bitter words and looks they exchange with Bengt's lawyer, Bertil Peyron.

The first person to give a witness statement this morning is Rut Sommer, Bengt's mother. She's made herself look nice. But it's still obvious that she's of a different class to, say, Margit Sivander. The suit wasn't tailored for her and fits a little awkwardly. Her shoes are polished, but worn. I follow her as she takes tiny steps to the witness chair. Rut squeezes her hands to keep them from shaking as she sits down. She holds her head high, the tendons of her neck are taut violin strings. No, it's me holding my head high, my blood pumping violently through the chambers of my heart. I'm Rut.

'How many children do you have, Mrs Sommer?'

'Three,' I answer. 'Two boys and a girl.'

The chairman lowers his head so that his eyebrows obscure his grey eyes.

'How big is your apartment?'

'One room and a kitchen downstairs, and one room upstairs,' I say, clearing my throat.

He asks me a lot of questions about our home. About the entrance, if there's a vestibule or hall, about the direction the house faces. Why this is important I don't really know, but I answer conscientiously. Then he wants to know what time we usually eat, how often Otto works the night shift, what time our boys go to sleep. I tell him mealtimes and bedtimes vary, it depends on whether Otto's working that night or not, whether it's summer or not. The chairman's eyebrows rise. It feels like he's come to pass judgment on me. I want him to understand I do have my principles. That's why I raise my chin even higher when I emphasise the importance of my boys eating well before bedtime.

'Mrs Sommer, would you be so kind as to tell us about the clothes Bengt was wearing on Friday the seventh of May?'

I feel like a good mother when I'm able to describe exactly what Bengt was wearing, and where and when each piece of Bengt's clothes had been bought.

'How long had he been wearing that shirt?'

But this question makes me shrink again. I feel ashamed.

'For over a week.'

The chairman glances in the direction of a man to his left. Their eyes mirror each other's, their gazes bouncing off the tabletop, conveying their mutual distrust.

'The jacket was bought in Helsingborg two years and five months ago, you said. Did he use it often?'

'Lately he's had it on every day.'

'And did you wash it sometimes?'

'I've never washed it, no.' The blood rushes to my face. But, I remind myself, it's important to tell the truth. Because of the stains. 'I've pressed it with a damp cloth, but never washed it.'

'You've never washed it. But did you ever remove any stains from it?'

My hands start to shake, and I squeeze them so hard my knuckles turn white.

'Yes, I have.'

'And his trousers were purchased after Christmas 1947. Have you washed them, then?'

'No.'

I wish he would change the subject.

'Tell me about the grey canvas shoes that Bengt wore during the evening in question.'

'Well, I think we bought them at the beginning of April this year. At Johan Nilsson's shoe store.' I sit up straighter. 'They were a bit more expensive than regular gym shoes, actually. They cost six kronor.'

'He has a pair of white ones, too. And you preferred he use those when he played football, because they were older?'

'Yes, but he didn't think they worked as well for kicking a ball.'

'And he got the white ones from his coach, Edvin Oskarsson.'

I sense a shift in the crowd behind me. Do they think this is odd?

'Yes . . .' I begin uncertainly. 'Yes, he came home with them one evening.'

It wasn't the first time that we've received clothes or shoes for the children. People can be so kind. But Bengt always disliked those shoes. I have never understood why. They're the same as the grey ones, how can there be such a big difference? My gaze drifts into the empty space behind the chairman until he clears his throat.

'Now, Mrs Sommer, I'd like to talk about that Friday. What time did Bengt leave home?'

'I remember precisely, because I'd just come home from town with a suit jacket and a pair of trousers for him. I'd been given the clothes by a lady I know. Because Siv, my daughter, was getting married. Yes, she got married at Whitsuntide. Neither I nor Bengt were at the wedding. Bengt was in custody, and I was . . .' I stare down miserably at my hands, trying to hold back my tears. I can't bring myself to say that I was in a psychiatric ward at that time. 'I told Bengt to try on the clothes, so I'd have time to repair a hole in one knee before the wedding. If they didn't fit, there was no point in fixing it.' I try not to talk too much or too fast. 'And then Bengt said we had to hurry because he was headed to practice. He tried on the clothes, and they fitted just right, he looked so handsome.' I look up and swallow. The ceiling is white and arched with heavy crystal chandeliers hanging from it. 'When he left the news had just been on, so it was ten or a quarter past seven.'

'When did he come home?'

'It was about a quarter past eight.'

'Mrs Sommer, you gave a different time to the police.'

'Did I?' I fall silent and try to think quickly. 'Yes, I can stretch it to between a quarter past eight and twenty past eight.'

'Did you tell that to the police?'

My whole body starts to vibrate, all the way to my fingertips. I think they can see it, my blouse shaking above my breast. What, what was it I said?

'I remember . . . I remember with *certainty* . . .' I emphasise that word, and say it again just in case. 'With *certainty* that Parish Constable Andersson asked me, when they picked up the shoes, if it might be possible that he came home as late as eight thirty. "Absolutely not," I said at the time.'

'What condition were Bengt's shoes in when he got home?'

193

'I remember where I was standing at the table . . .' I float away. I let go, fly out of that airless courtroom through the window. The sun is just peeking out through silvery clouds. I drown in the memory of that moment as I stand there at the table, in the anguish that's now seared into it. What happened has already happened. I want to lock Bengt away somewhere, where no one can ever find him. Suddenly, I remember him as a newborn. His silky head. Those tiny hands waving in the air. The little body that wanted only to be closer to mine. Defenceless. And completely innocent.

'Where? In the kitchen?'

The chairman's voice cuts through my visions and memories like a giant, rusty pair of scissors.

'Yes. Bengt stopped on the rug in the hall and said, "My shoes are dirty, Mama." I told him to take the brush from the cupboard and clean the shoes himself.'

I try to remember Bengt that evening. Surely, he was as always? Surely everything was? The chairman says something that I can't quite hear, I'm lost in the memory of my boys sitting at the top of the stairs. I surprised them with sweet buns. Then I washed their feet. The boys were talking about the match in Tyringe that Bengt was supposed to play in the next day. They were joking about how many goals Bengt would score. They put on their pyjamas. They look so cute in those. I tilt my head and smile.

'Did Bengt tell you where he'd been, if he'd been kicking a ball or practising?'

'No.'

'But Mrs Sommer, in the police report you said Bengt told you he'd been outside kicking a ball. Maybe they got it wrong, then?'

Kicking a ball. Practising. What difference does it make?

'*I* think the police could have said they had my boy. I only found out when my husband came home and told me. I couldn't believe it was true.'

194

Upset now, red splotches flare up from beneath my blouse, spreading onto my neck and chest.

'Mrs Sommer, were you familiar with Birgitta's appearance?'

I go still. I can see the girl's face in front of me.

'Yes.'

He stares at me silently for a moment, before speaking again. 'So, how did you hear about Birgitta's death?'

'That was on Saturday morning. My husband came home at six o'clock in the morning and woke me. He slowly said, "Can you imagine anything more awful."' You could have heard a pin drop in the courtroom. I'm silent for a long time, until the benches behind me start to creak as the audience shifts positions. '"Engineer Sivander's daughter has been murdered," he told me. "Her poor parents," I said. "Her poor parents."' I shake my head sadly. 'The boys woke up, and we went in to them. They asked, "What is it, Mama?" both at the same time. And we told them what happened.'

'How did Bengt react?'

'Not in any abnormal way.' I refuse to look up, not wanting to allow the chairman's piercing eyes to penetrate mine. 'I went down to the kitchen to make cocoa. And then Bengt told me he'd seen the girl down by the field the night before.'

'How would you describe Bengt's character? Is he soft, or hard?'

I see my son in front of me and imagine brushing the hair out of his eyes. And how, without changing his expression, he turns away from me, slams the front door behind him.

'Very soft.'

'Is he reserved?'

'Not towards me. He has always been open-hearted with me.'

I smooth out the folds of my skirt, and I'm struck by a dizzying realisation: this interrogation will never end; I am in hell.

'Bengt was in psychiatric care in Lund until the twenty-second of May. Where was he taken after that?'

'To my brother in Halmstad.'

My brother was angry when he called to tell me someone on the street recognised Bengt from that picture in the news-paper. They'd pushed my boy, screamed at him, chased him through the streets. My brother said Bengt was putting his family in danger by staying there. 'Is it possible . . .' I hesitate. 'Is it possible to take a break soon?'

'We'll soon be done, Mrs Sommer. Your husband is from the Sudetenland, and he's worked as an interpreter at his workplace. Do Germans often visit your home?'

'Yes.'

I shrink. Where is the chairman going with this?

'And these are people who experienced terrible things before they came to Sweden. Do they sometimes speak about it?'

'Yes, but we speak German to each other. The children don't know any German.' I run my fingertips lightly over my skirt, focusing on the texture.

'About a month ago, Bengt came home from your brother in Halmstad. How has he been since then? Has he been the same, do you think?'

'He didn't like having to stay inside when he got home. We received a very harsh statement from the Child Welfare Board. Both the boy and I started crying.'

I look around for compassion, but find none. I close my eyes and see the jurors' implacable faces in front of me. I remember how Bengt started breathing fast, shouting that he'd been arrested, that he was in prison. I had to hunch over as I made my way through town to do the shopping. Everyone was staring at me, whispering behind my back.

'I hardly recognised the boy the first few days after he came home. My daughter and son-in-law came to visit, and we sat at the kitchen table. Suddenly Bengt went over to my son-in-law and sat down next to him on the edge of the sofa. He was completely white. I saw it.' I stare blankly into the air, pressing

196

my fingertips to my temples. 'And I said, "But Bengt, are you okay?" He stared and . . . his eyes sort of rolled back, so only the whites were visible. My son-in-law threw his arms around him, because it looked like he was going to topple over. I went to them and put my hands around Bengt's shoulders and said, "Is there something you want to confess to your mother, Bengt?" But he said, "No, I haven't seen the girl." And then he grabbed his head and said, "But the cops are staring at me." The sweat just poured off him. "Don't leave me," Bengt begged. He said, "They're laughing at me, sneering. They're staring into my head. I can hear the policemen's voices all the time."'

With a long, shaky exhalation, I release my bone-tight grip on the edges of the chair and sink back against the back-rest.

'I crushed a sleeping pill into some milk and gave it to him.'

'How long did it take for him to recover?'

'A few days.'

It's dead silent in the courtroom for several seconds before I speak again.

'I think that I, as a mother,' I begin. 'That I, who gave birth to him, have the greatest right to ask him. I once said to him, "Bengt, now that we are alone." And I said, "You believe in God, don't you, Bengt? You must bear in mind that one day you will stand before him with Birgitta by your side, and you will have to answer for what you've done. Do you understand you will have to speak the truth?" And he said, 'Yes, Mama, but it wasn't me." And he looked me right in the eye.'

I come down after putting Vivi to bed to the sound of punching and kicking blaring from the living-room TV.

'Mum, I beat Dad!' I hear halfway down the stairs.

Sam, red-cheeked, is jumping up and down on the sofa with the video game controller in his hands. I look at the screen. Sam's avatar is an enormous, wolfish man with a wicked grin. Justus also has a muscular male avatar.

Justus surprised me with an excursion to Sturehov castle this morning, without the children. We left them at my parents' house and were gone for five hours. I took off my sandals in the car and turned up the volume on the radio. Freedom bloomed inside my chest, and the guitar string connecting me to Vivi was pulled so taut that if you ran straight into it, it would snap you in half. It was probably good for her. She's sleeping restlessly upstairs now, maybe because we've been apart.

'Mum, do you wanna watch?'

I can hear Sam doing his best to sound nonchalant, like it doesn't matter, but he really wants me to see. I don't want to, don't want to watch my son and his father thrash each other.

'I have some work to do,' I begin.

'Okay' he says sadly.

'But I'll be back soon. I just have to finish up,' I say.

In the kitchen, there's a child-sized black wooden chair behind the refrigerator. I sit there. No one can see me from anywhere in the apartment and I go there when I need to be alone. I scroll on my phone and eat a cookie. Sam and Justus make choked noises of frustration and joy to each other.

'Mum, can't you come soon?' Sam shouts. 'I'm winning!'

I chew before answering.

'That's fun! Yes, I will.'

I take a deep breath and stand up. I watch Sam as I head towards the couch; he's mirroring his avatar's movements: jumping, lunging. He's like an atomic bomb. An explosion. I don't even know how many times a day I have to say 'Watch out for Vivi!' But he is sweet, I know he is. He helps Vivi up when she falls, he holds her hand and leads her in the right direction when she toddles off, and he hugs her all the time. When, as usual, she falls and hurts herself, horror washes over Sam's face.

Now I settle down on the sofa next to Sam. Justus is sitting on the coffee table. Turning from Sam towards the screen, I watch as oversized men fight each other, while in the background three distorted female figures in bikinis sway this way and that.

'What the hell.'

I expel half a sentence, tired and resigned. Justus looks over his shoulder at me.

'What?'

I see Sam throw a worried look in my direction. He might as well have dropped to his knees and begged me to share something he likes with him. He wants me to be part of this. Feelings rise like water inside me, guilt for not being a part of this game and guilt for exposing him to this shit. Soon the feelings are up to my nose.

'How can you let him play stuff like this,' I say to Justus, in English so Sam won't understand.

'What?'

Can't he see it?

'This is violent, and super fucking sexist!'

Justus just shrugs. Doesn't he care? Does he think it doesn't mean anything? I start to boil inside. I want to cry. It feels like it's all a lie, like he's not really on my side, like all men are in league with each other. They want to pass on their violence and sexism to the next generation. Did I only imagine we discussed all this? Did I never make my boundaries clear?

'Are there no girls in this game? Besides the ones dancing in their underwear,' I say as sweetly as I can.

'Yeah, there are!'

Justus and Sam compete to see who can best assure me of that. The match ends. Justus won. He beat Sam.

'Real pumped-up girls, Mum!' Sam says while Justus goes into the character list to show me. Justus chooses a girl this time. Her face is expressionless, her eyes large and brown, her mouth inviting. Sam wants the same one as before, the supervillain. The girl is very muscular. Her thighs are powerful. Should this be enough for me? Is that where I set the bar? I feel like they're both waiting for some kind of approval while they play. I feel sick as I watch Sam's avatar kicking and punching Justus. The anatomically impossible girls dance in the background.

Two boys dressed in brown stand next to each other in the yard in front of their house. One is 8, the other 12. It's a misty autumn day in 1942, six years before Birgitta's murder. The tree branches hang heavy with fruit. A sweet smell of rotting apples permeates Perstorp. Opposite the two brothers stands Bengt. He's also 8. They've been playing all day, but now the older brother and Bengt are arguing about something. Afterwards, no one can remember how it started. The air between them is charged. The little brother is amused by the drama and smiles playfully, while both the big brother and Bengt are panting with anger. It's cold enough to turn their breath to clouds.

'You look like dragons,' the little brother laughs.

His older brother picks up a stone and throws it at Bengt, or was it Bengt who threw a rock first? Neither hits its target. Then the big brother throws his arms wide in frustration and turns around. Bengt picks something up from the ground and throws again. It hits the big brother in the back of the head. Now the little brother's smile disappears. His brother sinks to the ground. Blood starts to gush immediately.

'Help!' shouts the little brother. 'Help!'

The brother-in-law of the two brothers rushes out the front door. He falls to his knees next to the eldest, who is breathing rapidly. Something is sticking out of the back of his head. The brother-in-law stares at the object in bewilderment.

'Sit very still now,' he says and raises his hand.

But the boy flinches.

'What is that?' he says, with horror in his voice.

The brother-in-law looks at the younger of the brothers, and then at Bengt.

'What did you do?'

His accusation causes Bengt to falter. His eyes are wide, and he's staring at the blood running down the big brother's shirt, sticking it to his back. Shoulder blades rise and fall rapidly beneath it. Then the brother-in-law puts a hand on the big brother's shoulder. He holds him tight, and with a quick movement, the brother-in-law grabs the object and pulls it out. The younger brother blanches as the elder screams. The brother-in-law holds up the object and twists and turns it in puzzlement. It's a piece of a scythe, about twenty centimetres long. He lays it down on the grass and sits down next to the big brother, lifting his hair to examine the wound.

'Am I going to die?' the boy sobs.

The brother-in-law can see now that the wound isn't very deep.

'No, you're not.'

He pats the boy on the shoulder and stands up, ready to lecture Bengt. But he's already gone.

It's late at night when I open the court records again. I'm pushing at them like a door, but a silence seems to separate me from the moment in which they were written. I try to imagine Bengt's father on the witness stand, but my eyes sting with fatigue.

'My name is Otto Sommer, and I was born in Weisswasser in Germany. I came to Sweden in 1924, and I've lived in Perstorp ever since.'

What does his voice sound like? Is he trying to sound as Swedish as possible?

The chairman asks if Otto remembers what Birgitta looked like, and Otto tells him he's only seen her once. It was when she came to the factory to raise money for charity. Birgitta appears before his eyes carrying a box full of fabric flowers for sale. Like a will-o'-the-wisp hovering among the men in the factory. That year the flowers were white with a yellow centre.

I wonder if Otto is prepared for the chairman's next question. I'm guessing he is; questions about their family life always end up here.

'Do you have foreigners at your home sometimes?'

'Yes. My countrymen.'

The chairman asks if they talk about their experiences with the horrors of war. They do, but not so the children can hear, Otto answers, just like Rut.

It's much easier to imagine Otto in the small kitchen of the Sommers' home than in court. The faces bent over the kitchen table, hands clasped and voices whispering. The serious faces of the boys as they eavesdrop from the top of the stairs, as children always do.

The chairman asks about Bengt's character, whether it could be described as weak and soft, or hard. Otto replies that Bengt gets tears in his eyes if spoken to sharply, or when he gets hit. His answer leads the chairman to the next question: what is Otto like as a family man? Does he reason with his children or does he use other means? It's an important question. I know what the chairman is getting at – children learn what is considered acceptable behaviour towards others from the adults around them. If Bengt has been exposed to violence, then it's more likely he'll use violence to resolve a conflict.

'My children are expected to behave. They're not allowed to do as they please,' Otto says.

The chairman takes one step closer to the heart of the matter.

'Do you discipline you children?'

The question is being asked at a time when corporal punishment is still legal in Sweden. Many consider a certain amount of physical discipline a necessary element of child-rearing. But there are still limits.

'It happens,' replies Otto.

'Does Bengt ever talk about girls?' wonders the chairman.

'No. He barely even dares look at them,' says Otto.

It's half a year before Birgitta's murder and the ice shines atop Perstorp's pond. The sixth graders are skating. One girl is gliding around and around the edge of the pond. Her dark hair curls beneath a snug cap, and her round face shines like the moon. She's on her own, skating and daydreaming. Then a boy slides in front of her, his cheeks red. A short, blonde fringe sticks straight up below the brim of his cap, and his smile is wide. It's Bengt. He's 14, and the girl, Barbro, is 12. He skates backwards in front of her, smiling. Barbro tries to dart past him, but he skids in front of her, and she almost falls. He forces her to stop.

'Can you come out tonight?' he asks.

Bengt is too close. It makes Barbro nervous, confused. All her friends are girls of the same age as her. Bengt has never said a word to her before. Barbro vaguely senses that her mother wouldn't approve.

'No, I'm going home,' she says.

Barbro catches a friend's eye to ask for help.

'Some other time then?'

Bengt's grin is still just as wide. His teeth glint in the sun.

'You're crazy,' she says, heading sharply to the right and arcing around him.

Ella Jonsson, the Sommer family's neighbour, raises her eyebrows meaningfully as she looks at the chairman. She's wearing the same dark dress she wore to Birgitta's funeral. Her substantial bosom lifts as she straightens her back, and her painted lips stretch like a rubber band into a wide smile.

Ella has just testified about a day last winter when she went over to the Sommer family to wish them Merry Christmas. While sitting with Rut in the kitchen, Bengt's little brother, Axel, had come in. He put his arms around his mother's neck and whispered something, and Rut laughed. 'He says he's got a fiancée,' she explained to Ella. Then Bengt popped in. He leaned against the door-frame and said teasingly: 'Oh yeah, you getting married, Axel?' Axel replied quickly that Bengt had a fiancée too. 'Birgitta.'

'And you're sure he said Birgitta?' the chairman asks.

'I'm sure.'

Her voice is somehow both chirpy and deep. Ella's hands sit clasped in her lap above an imaginary purse. The chairman smiles quickly and continues.

'How would you describe Bengt's character?'

'Well, the boy is a sweetie. That's what I think,' Ella replies and tilts her head, pursing her lips.

'How does he treat his parents, his mother?'

'That's hard to say.' Ella glances up at the ceiling, pulling her mouth to one side. 'She's said he can get a little short with her. Not like Axel. But I've always found him sweet.'

'Did he ignore his mother?'

'Well, perhaps, but you know what children that age are like.'

She widens her smile again, about to start a story about her own son at that age, but is interrupted. Ella takes a deep breath, trying her best to hide how much she dislikes having someone else steer the conversation.

'Mrs Jonsson, do you think he felt sorry for his mother?'

Ella narrows her grey-blue eyes at the chairman.

'No.'

'Is his mother sick?'

'Well, it's her nerves.'

'Is she annoyed and troubled?'

'Yes.'

'But Bengt doesn't feel compassion for his mother.'

'His mother says not.'

'That Bengt doesn't care about her?'

'Rut said he was hard. Not like Axel at all. He's so hard, she said.'

It's the final day of the trial. A line of nervous children is photographed by reporters as they file into the courtroom. The door closes behind them. Today's hearing will take place behind closed doors, because of the age of the witnesses. Most are boys, the ones who were on the football field the evening of the murder. Karl is among them. Three of the children are girls. One is Barbro, the girl on the ice. The other two are named Britta and Anita. Their stories are highlighted in order to say something negative about Bengt's character, along with the incident when Bengt threw the piece of a scythe at another boy, at age 8. But no witnesses to that incident are heard in court.

February 1948. Two girls are outside playing, three months before the murder of their schoolmate. Britta, age 12, and her friend Anita, age 9. It's close to seven o'clock in the evening, and pitch-black outside. They take turns on the swing. Right now, it's Anita's turn. Britta is squatting down in front of a rabbit cage, shoving pieces of dried grass inside. Two soft, rounded bunnies hop around, uninterested in what she has to offer.

'We're moving next week,' says Britta. 'To Spjutseröd.'

Anita stretches her feet forward like an arrow while leaning far back in order to gather speed. Now they hear something bouncing, and Britta looks in the direction it's coming from. Anita stops pumping her feet.

'Who is it?' she asks.

'It's Bengt.' The Sommer family have lived next door to Britta's family most of her life. 'His little brother is in my class.'

Bengt is bouncing a ball on the street as he strolls towards the girls. Britta stands up. He's never said a word to her before. Now he stares at Anita for a long time, then at Britta.

'Should we go to the woods and screw?' he says.

Britta has only the fuzziest idea of what that means. She blushes deeply and lowers her eyes.

'You're so immature, Bengt,' she says.

'Yeah, so immature!' Anita echoes.

Britta can see Anita doesn't know what Bengt is referring to. Bengt shrugs and continues bouncing his ball. It's no fun to keep playing now. Both Britta and Anita feel like they're being watched. Soon, Anita heads home. Britta remains on the swing scraping her feet against the ground. Out of the corner of her eye, she can see Bengt coming towards her again.

'Are you gonna watch the game tonight?'

'No,' Britta says, shaking her head without looking up.

Bengt shrugs and starts walking home again. Britta stays on the swing, listening to the bouncing of a ball until it stops.

In the evening, I take out the only picture I have of Bengt. The one printed in the newspaper. His blonde hair sticks straight up. He's laughing, his teeth gappy and childishly oversized. I stare into his eyes for a long time. Is there any way to see who he was, or is? I can't grasp him through his interrogations. He sounds like a typical teenager to me. But parents don't know everything there is to know about their children. In one way they do, but in another they know nothing at all. The boys in Bengt's class all agreed that he was a nice kid. Apart from Barbro, Britta and Anita, no other girls were interviewed. Ella stated that Rut called Bengt hard, 'not at all like Axel'. But Rut says the opposite, she calls him soft in court. In and of itself, it wouldn't be strange if Bengt was tougher than his brother. Axel was still a child, while Bengt was a teenager. Teenagers tend to be harsh towards a weak mother. Because they can, because they know she'll still be there even if they slam a door in her face. Or was there something more? Did Rut see a darkness in her son, and confide in her neighbour?

Karl sits on his hands, looking down. The chairman's chair creaks as he leans forward.

'What grade are you in?'

Karl answers quietly. The chairman asks him to speak up.

'Fifth grade. I'm starting sixth after summer break.'

'Do you remember what you did on the evening your sister disappeared?'

'After dinner I played with Åke and a few others. We went to a building by the old football field and climbed in through the window.'

'And after that you went to kick a ball. Was that when you saw Birgitta?'

Karl squirms. The people in the rows behind him stare at his back, their eyes follow each breath, and without being conscious of it, they begin to breathe in time with him.

'She walked by. And stopped at the entrance.'

'Do you know Bengt Sommer?'

'Yes.'

'Was he there too?'

'Yes. All three of them stood talking. Åke, Birgitta and Bengt. But I don't know if Birgitta said anything. Åke asked Bengt if he wanted to kick a ball with us, but he said he was going home to eat.'

'Did you hear that?'

'Yeah, we asked him twice.' Karl meets the chairman's eyes for the first time. His own are flat and serious, like an adult's. 'Then Sonja came. By then Birgitta was walking home.'

'How was Birgitta dressed?'

'I don't remember.'

'What kind of socks was she wearing?'

Karl stares, uncomprehendingly, at the chairman. He shakes his head.

'I don't know. White, I think.'

The chairman changes the subject.

'Did Birgitta play with dolls?'

'Not so much anymore,' replies Karl.

'Did she think it was more fun to play with boys?'

'Don't know.'

Karl's cheeks turn faintly pink. It's all a silly little dance. Somewhere he can hear his father sighing.

'Did Birgitta say she wanted to get married someday?' continues the chairman, pretending no one knows where he's going with this.

'She told me when she grew up she was going to marry Yngve.'

'Not anyone else?'

'When we played with Axel, she wanted to marry him. Axel Sommer.'

I've decided to start meditating to calm myself down. I have been living and breathing police interrogations, court records and autopsy reports for so long now. It feels like I'm approaching my limits. In the evening I go up to my study, lie down on the rug and start a guided meditation. But when I try to relax, all I can feel is how thirsty I am, how dry my lips are, how much I need to pee. I give up and go watch TV with Justus until it's time for bed.

I fall asleep, and Birgitta arrives. She holds out a sprig of dried lavender and a folded piece of paper. There is an eight drawn on it, in soft pencil. She tells me to burn it. It's like a spell. What does it mean? Lavender symbolises calm, silence, sleep. The eight could also be a B, as in Birgitta, before it falls and flattens. Eight is four plus four; Birgitta was murdered in 1948. Perhaps Birgitta is the number eight.

I tell Justus about the dream in the morning, and we laugh. In the evening, I light a fire, and once it gets going, I rummage through the junk drawer for a piece of paper. I write an eight on it and take a dried sprig of lavender from a vase in the kitchen window. When Justus isn't looking, I throw them both into the fire. I watch as they start to glow, burn and finally turn to ash.

In the evening, I listen to a guided meditation again. I'm wearing a sleep mask and lie awake for a long time with my eyes staring into the blackness. Shadows and dots start to play in front of me after a while. I can't grasp them. I try to fix my gaze, but the shapes keep changing, like a mass of pine cone scales, growing and folding outwards. It must be around the moment I fall asleep that I finally make out a shape emerging from its centre – a conifer cone.

Valdemar is dressed in a well-tailored suit. The dark shadows on his face lend it a melancholy air.

'I'd like to know more about your daughter,' the chairman says. 'Would you consider Birgitta mentally competent for her years? Or was she immature?'

'She was exactly as a 9-year-old should be,' answers Valdemar quietly. 'She liked talking to the people she knew. She was high-spirited.'

'Did your daughter have any special interests?'

The chairman tilts his heavy head. Valdemar's eyes are shiny. When he blinks, a tear slips out. He quickly wipes it away.

'She loved picking flowers in the spring. Every day. On her own. Once, she found some lilies of the valley blooming early and told some of her friends about it. But they told all the other girls in her class, and it upset her very much.'

'Was she easy to tempt, Mr Sivander? If you were to promise her chocolate or sweets, for example.'

'I find it hard to imagine she would ever follow someone she didn't know.'

'Did she go to the football field often?'

'She and I used to go run on the track there together,' says Valdemar, closing his eyes and lowering his face to his shoulder, as if toward an invisible cheek.

'Was she a romantic by nature?'

Valdemar straightens again and stares hard at the chairman.

'Romantic? In what respect?'

'Did she have any interest – did she show signs of affection in some way that took a more . . .' The chairman gropes for the right words. '. . . pronounced expression?'

'We have a 1-year-old she liked to hug,' answers Valdemar.

Their eyes size each other up. The chairman sighs. A pattering of rain starts against the window.

Elin Sjöberg's round, broad shoulders look heavy. Her eyelashes are transparent and straight. Elin's body is marked by her pregnancies and hard physical labour, her hands are rough and dry, and cracks in her skin run like thin, black veins of earth that cannot be washed away. She read in the newspaper that the primary witnesses were to be heard today. At first, she thought that included her, but it didn't. They were referring to the Sommer family's neighbour Roland Nilsson and sports director Edvin Oskarsson.

'Mrs Sjöberg, is it correct that you made certain observations on the evening that Birgitta disappeared?'

Elin is startled. She didn't know that the interrogation would start so suddenly, without any greetings.

'Yes, that's right,' she answers.

'And Mrs Sjöberg, you are married to . . .' The chairman lifts up a piece of paper and reads with narrowed eyes. '. . . Holger Sjöberg, farmer. You have a farm at the base of the forest where the girl was found.'

'Yes, my husband leases the land.'

'Mrs Sjöberg, could you tell us about what you saw from your vegetable garden, the man coming down from the forest. How far away was he?'

'About two hundred metres. He walked into the clearing by the river that runs nearby, at the edge of the forest,' answers Elin.

'Which direction is that?'

Elin shrugs apologetically.

'Compass directions aren't my strong suit. But from where I stood, the forest lay directly in front of me, and the football field down to the right. If you follow the river, you'll get there.'

'What did the man look like?'

'He was wearing black swimming trunks or something like them. He had dark hair, or maybe a black beret.'

'Paint the scene for us, exactly how you saw it.'

'Well,' Elin says and straightens up. 'It was about a quarter to eight. The last bit of sun was shining down on the man. So I could see him very clearly. I'd guess he was about 175 centimetres tall.' Elin falls silent, but when the chairman asks no further questions, she continues. 'There's no road or path in that direction, so I almost never see people there.'

Especially not half-naked ones, Elin thinks.

'He was headed towards the football field. And I remember thinking that was very strange,' she continues. 'When I went inside, I immediately told my husband about it. And then later we heard what happened . . .' Elin's eyes fill with tears. 'The little girl was friends with our St Bernard. And he went completely crazy that evening. Barking at the forest until after nine o'clock. Later I started to realise . . .'

'The wind was blowing from the north-west. You can very well imagine that the dog heard screams you might not have perceived.'

'Yes,' says Elin and nods, 'I think that's right.'

'The dog knew Birgitta, you said. Did Birgitta visit you often?'

'Yes, she came by a lot, so she knew our dog very well.'

When Elin is on the train headed home from the Klippan courthouse, she feels pleased with her contribution. She tells Holger about it at the dinner table late that evening, and he pats her on the shoulder.

'You did good, Elin.'

A few days later, a neighbour arrives with a copy of the *Dagens Nyheter* paper.

'Mrs Sjöberg, you're in the newspaper today!' she shouts happily over the grass.

Elin brushes her hands on the apron and grabs the newspaper to read it aloud.

'*"The Beret Man" in Perstorp that the witness E Sjöberg saw walking into the forest beyond the old football field* – no, no, it was out of the forest – *is one of the many unresolved details. The National Criminal Police did everything they could to confirm whether he really existed* – oh, they did, did they – *or if the witness is guilty . . .*'

Elin's voice starts to fade away. She reads the rest silently.

. . . of constructing all this in hindsight. The police didn't come into contact with Mrs Sjöberg until three weeks after the murder. Even if one of the athletes training on the football field on that fateful Friday night took a run across the springy meadow where she claims to have observed this man, it does not necessarily mean it's connected to the murder.

Elin looks up from the newspaper, towards the dense forest. 'Springy meadow,' she repeats silently to herself. She presses the newspaper back into her neighbour's chest, trudges into her house and kicks off her shoes.

In an interview on 24 July, two weeks after Elin Sjöberg's testimony, Senior Constable Björn Gerell tells *Dagens Nyheter*: *Finally, I can now announce that the mysterious man in a beret and swimming trunks, allegedly seen near the scene of the murder, has been identified as an orienteer and removed from suspicion.* Why was he removed? Did he have the wrong shoe size, perhaps? The orienteer isn't mentioned elsewhere in the investigation, despite the fact that he was surely in the forest at the time of the murder. Shouldn't his testimony be of interest to the police? He could have seen or heard something, if nothing else. I find it so odd.

One evening I'm lying in bed reading posts in the Perstorp Facebook group. A woman has posted a black and white picture from the Perstorp sports club taken in 1959. It depicts ten young men, smiling in white shirts, and one man in a dark polo shirt standing in the middle. In the caption, the club's fight song is quoted. It begins: *Sports Club Boys are unstoppable and all resistance falls*. I'm startled to see the name Axel Sommer. Bengt's little brother. He must have been 23 when the picture was taken; he has a boyish, puppyish look and a slim build. His hair stands straight up. At the time the picture was taken, Bengt no longer lived in Perstorp. He had already moved to the address where he's still registered today. My gaze drifts to the left of the image. The team coach, a bit stocky with a dark jacket over his suit, stands there with his hands clasped over his stomach. He smiles crookedly, a black beret balanced on his head. The man is Edvin Oskarsson.

Another person has posted some newspaper clippings about Birgitta's murder. On one of the clippings there's an image of a woman in motion, dressed in a light skirt and dark cardigan. The caption tells us she found 'a new piece of evidence' – a beret in the forest. The article is from *Stockholms-Tidningen* on 11 May. The beret was found two days after the murder, in the woods a few hundred metres from the crime scene. The man Elin saw had very dark hair or was wearing a beret. In almost every picture of Edvin Oskarsson before the murder, he's wearing a black beret. In the photos immediately after the murder, when he's being interviewed or testifying in court, he wears no beret. His dark hair is slicked back. Maybe the beret was more of a casual garment? Not something you wore when you were photographed in a serious setting? Or, could he have buried his bloody clothes in the forest, lost his beret, then come down into the clearing where Elin Sjöberg saw him? But then how did he do it? Where did he get the new clothes, and how did he make it back to his bike, which still stood at the football field? Could he have slipped back unseen, changed clothes in the dressing room and cycled away? Maybe, but it would be strange that no one saw him.

It's a lovely day. Sunny and not freezing. I take the pushchair, and I'm surprised by how calm Vivi is in it. She holds her little toy cat tight in one fist, while dozing against the back-rest.

'We can go to the church and light some candles,' I tell Vivi, who looks back lazily. When I make a right toward the church, I get lost and end up at a park instead. One word on a sign catches my attention: 'Larch'. They grow here. Birgitta asked her teacher if there were larch trees growing above the old football field on the day she was murdered. Now my eyes drift across the park in search of pink cones and sweeping clusters of needles stretching up into the sky. I walk up a dirt path, follow it throughout the park as I search for them, but all the trees are brown, black and grey. Vivi falls asleep.

First I find only pines. I take out my phone and search for pictures of larch trees and discover that, unlike many conifers, they change colour in the autumn and lose their needles in the winter; they are deciduous. As soon as I look up from my screen, I see several. Their branches are narrow and prickly, the cones small and hard with holes in them. I snap off two. I sense a shadow in the corner of my eye. Birgitta is standing there. I turn and hold out the twigs.

As we approach the church, a chainsaw starts to roar. A man is trimming bushes right in front of the church. He meets my gaze, but his eyes seem empty. Maybe we're not supposed to go into the church today, but I'm headed in anyway. Vivi turns restlessly in her sleep as we pass by him. Just as I'm about to enter, two men in dark suits come out. One carries a bouquet under his arm and they've both been crying. I nod apologetically, keep my eyes low and half turn towards the shadow at my side. I'll be better at listening next time.

The trees rustle as Otto Sommer makes his way home from his shift at the factory. It feels like he's sinking into the asphalt, as if soon he won't be able to go on, he'll be crushed into the pavement. But still, each step carries him relentlessly closer to home. As Otto turns up his street, he can see the reporters and curious onlookers lined up along his fence.

Otto passes by them without a glance in their direction. He walks through his little garden. The brass handle on his door is shiny and worn. He notes how he's breathing through his nose, light and shallow. Then he turns the handle and steps into the darkness.

It's like opening the door to an atomic nucleus. He can feel the rushing energy, the madness, the buzzing, all at an impossible speed. Somewhere in there his wife is screaming, somewhere his daughter is crying. Bengt is at some facility; Otto doesn't remember which one now, and he keeps mixing them up. Axel sits on a chair in the kitchen. His knees are pressed to his chest, and his arms are wrapped around them. Otto pulls a chair up beside him. He puts a hand on his son's shoulder. A tremor rolls through his small body. Otto notices the dirty dishes that fill the sink and cover the counter. The piles of torn letters on the floor.

'No one . . . wants . . .' Axel sobs.

Otto pats him awkwardly on the back, pats him a few times.

'They say . . . that . . . they don't wanna be around . . . the brother of . . . a murderer.'

The words tumble out in spurts. Otto presses his hands to the sides of Axel's head while pushing his own face against his son's knees and crossed arms. Otto gives in and starts to weep with him.

I remember exactly when Sam learned to crawl. Ever since, he's been on his way away from me. I would gather him into my arms and sit on the sofa and he would rock his whole body in a struggle to get free. I'd put him down on the floor, and he'd crawl away. I sometimes thought I'd never be allowed to hold him again. I was so careful not to force myself on him. I wanted to respect his bodily autonomy, so he'd do the same to other people in the future. In retrospect, I've wondered if I turned physical proximity into something nervous and strange. He's not particularly cuddly.

Vivi is. She's been crawling for months now and still wants to be held constantly. Cuddles and snuggling up close. But Sam still very much needs you to be present. If you watch a movie with him, you can't take your eyes off the screen. He makes sure you're watching every fun or exciting thing that might happen. That's his version of closeness. But it's not mine, and I often end up frustrated. I want to be close while doing different things. I'd like to sit back-to-back, while one reads and the other draws. It's not easy to find mutual ground.

When I go downstairs after getting Vivi to sleep, Sam's already gone up to bed. The second I set foot on the bottom step I hear his voice.

'Dad!' he shouts.

I hold a hand up to Justus, who was just standing up.

'I'll go.'

You can't help being reminded of a younger version of Sam as you approach his room; a picture from his old preschool

226

hangs on his door. In it he's smiling shyly, his hair curling. Even though he's still a kid, he feels like a mini-teenager now.

'What do you need, Sam?'

He raises himself on one arm.

'I wonder if, I don't remember if . . . Did I already get water?'

I can see the mug on his desk, a few drops still at the bottom.

'Yes,' I say. 'But I'm glad you shouted, because now I get to say goodnight.'

Sam sits up in the bunk bed, and I climb on the chair to reach him. He puts his arms around my neck; I put mine around his back. I hold tight with my lips pressed against his hair. The embrace lasts a long time, probably a whole minute. He's completely still. This almost never happens. Usually he's in constant motion. He sits on your lap and fidgets so much that a coffee mug overturns. He kisses hard and fast and repeatedly, like it's a game. But now everything is completely still, as if frozen in time. In the end, I'm the one who breaks contact, embarrassed by his sincerity. It feels unusual.

'Head on your pillow now,' I say.

The foyer of Perstorp's hotel smells of coffee and something vaguely chemical. The large, round lamp hanging from the ceiling sways back and forth. Dr Birger Sjödén is dressed in a light Fresco suit, carrying a briefcase in shiny, dark leather. His chin is pressed down into his neck, and his gaze fixed straight ahead. He's tired; the meeting with the Child Welfare Board didn't end until after midnight, and it didn't accomplish a damn thing. But it will be interesting to meet the boy; it always is. Bengt is an enigma, a tough nut to crack. Dr Sjödén has met all kinds of boys – neurotic, sickly, talented, nasty. At the Lövsta Reformatory, where he's the director, most of the boys can be placed into one of two categories. The first are the strong, rugged, violent boys. The second are the psychopaths.

Bengt he can't figure out. That fact that he so adamantly denies the accusations levelled against him suggests psychopathy, *if* he's the culprit. A normal 14-year-old would not be able to withstand the pressure of lengthy, repeated interrogations if he was guilty. Bengt has no history of violence or manipulation, except for that single episode where he angrily threw a piece of a scythe at another child. But he was only 8 at the time. Two men raise their hats in greeting as Dr Sjödén passes by on the sidewalk, but receive no response.

The streets are named for professions. The people living here are all working class. Low wooden fences surround tiny gardens. Rose hips and lemon-balm, potatoes and carrots grow in them. The bachelors' houses have only grass growing out front. The houses aren't that small, but often several families live crammed together in each one. Dr Sjödén hadn't known that when he came to visit the Sommer family for the first time, and he'd knocked on the wrong door. A large, burly woman in an apron had opened the door and sized him up, then leaned out and pointed around the corner.

When the doctor turns onto the Sommers' street today, he sees the usual gaggle of reporters in front of their house. They're clustered together, talking and laughing, cigarettes cradled in their hands or tucked behind their ears, butts scattered around them on the ground. The smell of a hangover wafts past the doctor as he passes by them. Several nod and mutter good morning, and one rushes over.

'Do you have time for a question, Doctor?'

'Well, that depends,' replies Dr Sjödén, but he stops and looks at the man.

'I understand there was a meeting last night.'

'Yes, that's correct.'

'Did you arrive at any conclusion?'

The other reporters have gathered in a crescent around them. The doctor looks them in the eye, one by one.

'No, no decision was made. My conversations with the boy will continue. Personally, I see no other solution than to entrust this investigation to a trained child psychiatrist rather than the Child Welfare Board, who lack expertise in this area. I'm convinced it would be best for all parties concerned. As you know, this case is not solely concerned with the conviction of a criminal.'

'Then what is it concerned with?'

A thin, middle-aged man with a receding hairline asks this question. He stares critically at Dr Sjödén, who calmly meets his gaze.

'There's also the matter of the authorities' obligation to guide a young boy.'

The first reporter raises his pen to indicate another question. He looks very young. Childish freckles are splashed across his nose. He might as well be one of the doctor's patients.

'Dr Torsten Thysell described the suspect as "a delightful boy". Do you share Dr Thysell's opinion?'

Dr Sjödén pinches his lips together.

'I think it would be inappropriate for me to answer that question.'

The grass in front of the Sommers' house is prickly and brown, the stairs grey and weathered. An enormous honeysuckle plant winds from the railing up to the wall. It almost looks like it's holding this house and its stairs together with coarse stitches.

Dr Sjödén gives three determined knocks on the door. Nothing happens for a while. After a while he can hear steps, and someone unlocks the door. It opens just a few centimetres, and inside it's dark.

'It's me, Dr Sjödén,' says the doctor.

A pale hand opens the door for him to enter. The doctor meets Rut Sommer's haggard face.

'How are you holding up, Mrs Sommer? I heard that . . .'

Sjödén falls silent when Rut looks at him. Her eyes are grey as thunderclouds.

'If it weren't for the fact that my son is going to be taken from me forever any day now, if our mailbox wasn't overflowing with letters from hypnotists and quacks, if I was able to go to the grocery store without my neighbours pointing and whispering, if I had been able to attended my daughter's wedding, if my little boy didn't come home crying from school every day, and if it weren't for these interrogations that just never end even though the trial is over, well then I would be just fine, thank you very much. Unfortunately, we can't offer you anything, because I haven't been able to do the shopping.'

Rut spat out the words. They stare at each other for a long second.

'I'm just trying to understand the boy,' says Dr Sjödén.

Rut snorts and leads him into the living room. Mummified porcelain flowers and African violets stand on the windowsills. On the dark green sofa, Bengt sits with his neck bent down towards hands that are clasped between his knees. Dr Sjödén smiles and settles gently into the armchair beside the sofa.

'Well, Bengt,' he says softly and opens his briefcase to take out his notepad. 'Did you have any more dreams since the last time we spoke?'

On 16 August 1998, the body of 4-year-old Kevin Hjalmarsson is found on a pallet in the reeds in Kyrkviken, Arvika. Initially, it's considered an accidental drowning, but during Kevin's autopsy, injuries are found that indicate something else. In the report from the National Crime Agency, it states that Kevin was probably choked to death – by a person who was not very strong.

Kevin's best friend, a boy of 5, enters the station. He had said something to his mother that makes her think he may have seen something. His big brother, aged 7, is at home. He's jealous. He wants to be part of this circus as well. Soon he's sitting in an interrogation room too. I watch parts of the boys' interrogations in a 2017 documentary called *The Kevin Case*. The 5-year-old can't sit still. He eagerly tells them all about things other than his friend's death, stumbling over the words. The 7-year-old presses himself against his mother, into her arms. My heart feels heavy when I see how small they both were. I can see Sam in both of them, and in Kevin.

According to the guidelines at the time, interrogations of children under 10 were supposed to be short, a maximum of half an hour long, and ideally there should have been no more than one. The questions were supposed be open, and the children were not supposed to be offered bribes. But these two brothers were interrogated a total of 31 times. Several of the interrogations lasted for more than an hour. They were threatened and bribed. The most heartbreaking scene was when the police promised one boy he would soon get to see his mother, as long as he answered 'correctly'. When one of them answered 'correctly', they were praised. The questions were closed and leading, and the police pitted the boys against each other.

Psychology professor Sven Å. Christianson was hired by the police as an adviser and became deeply involved in the investigation. He was familiar with the Mary Bell case. On 25 May 1968, the day before her eleventh birthday, Mary murdered 4-year-old Martin Brown in an abandoned house. Two months later, she took the life of 3-year-old Brian Howe. Brian was found between two large concrete blocks, covered in grass and weeds. I read quite a bit about Mary Bell; her childhood seems like a perfect recipe for the creation of a dangerous human being. She suffered abandonment, physical assault and sexual abuse. Mary Bell quickly transformed into myth, an evil child, almost inhuman, a demon. But the explanation for some of what she did was right there, for anyone who wanted to see it, in her childhood.

When I see those boys from Arvika sitting with their parents in the police's videotaped interrogation, I think of what the doctor who examined Vivi's heart said:

'This is not a heart-diseased child – children with a heart disease don't look like this.'

Can't they see it in that happy 5-year-old and shy 7-year-old, that they're healthy? Surely children who murder don't behave with such trust towards their parents, they don't move and talk like that? And they weren't guilty, after all. On 27 March 2018, the brothers were completely cleared of suspicion, and in March 2022 they were awarded damages of 1 million kronor each.

The boys are grown up now. They chose to take part in the documentary on Swedish public television, revealing both their names and their faces. In November 2020, they were also interviewed in an episode of *Framgångspodden*. I listen to it on the subway home from the National Library, standing outside our door with the key in my hand to finish it. One of the brothers says that Kevin was seen with a 13-year-old on the day he died. The 13-year-old was suspected of sexually abusing children both before and after. He sounds like the sort of person whose activities should have been investigated at the time of Kevin's death. Did the police ever do so?

Based on what I know about Bengt, he seems to have been healthy. There's no indication that he was physically or sexually abused. His classmates described him as nice. Do healthy children really kill? I begin to wonder: could there have been anyone else in Perstorp at the time of the murder whose background resembled that of Mary Bell?

I'm having a nightmare. A friend of Sam's is coming over for a sleepover. He's a little older than Sam. Once he arrives, he only wants to be alone in Sam's room with the door closed. Sam doesn't want to play with him either. I watch shadows seep from beneath the crack under the door, and darkness blinking in front of the keyhole as the boy moves on the other side. I know he's watching us. He steps out once and asks where Vivi is. I lie and say I don't know. He goes back in and closes the door behind him. Later, the door slams open and the boy walks toward me. I'm afraid of him but pretend to be caring and maternal. His hair is matted and dirty. I move my hands towards it as if to touch him, but I don't dare. Soon his parents are coming to pick him up, and I'm afraid they'll think we're bad adults for letting him get so dirty.

'You should probably take a shower,' I say, 'or a bath, if you like?'

The boy lunges at me. He tears and claws at my stomach while shouting 'Let me in! Let me in! You have to let me in!'

I back away from him in terror, and he stops, staring at me with a blank face, then walks back into Sam's room and shuts the door softly.

A moment later I wonder where Vivi is. I open the door to Sam's room and Vivi is lying on the floor, asleep. The boy is sitting on Sam's bed, staring down at me. I look up at him, eyes wide in horror as I lift Vivi's limp body. Cradling her in my arms, I back out and close the door. Then I go and lay Vivi in our bed. She's still sleeping.

'What if he did something to her . . .'

I wake up in a cold sweat, heart pounding. It takes me a long time to realise it wasn't real. I can't shake the feeling that an evil being has been trying to climb into me. At breakfast, I order a security alarm for the front door.

We eat as soon as Sam gets home from preschool. When we finish, it's still light outside. I tell Justus I'm headed out for a walk.

I pull on a fleece. The weather's mild and sunny, and the trees glimmer green. I walk up the wooded hill that runs next to the local football field, choose the path to the right. It's quiet up here, except for the distant sound of people kicking a ball about. And the music of an ice cream truck. Safe sounds.

I arrive at a small marsh. Not much more than a hollow really. It's full of dead logs and branches. The water is the clear brown of a beer bottle. It ripples on the surface almost imperceptibly. At the bottom, you can see yellow birch leaves. Suddenly, a wave of nausea washes into my throat and I have to hang my head between my knees. The wind picks up, and dry leaves rustle as they pass over ochre-coloured needles. I close my eyes and sit down on a mossy rock. After a while, I stand up and examine it. It's about the same size as the biggest stone Birgitta was buried beneath. I look around and see nobody, so I wrap my arms around the rock and try to lift it. It doesn't move a millimetre. It has to be stuck, I think, so I go to another rock. I can't lift that one up either. I try stone after stone. Only one do I manage to lift. It's about forty by fifteen centimetres. Surely, I can't be that weak? I can carry a child who weighs almost ten kilograms for several hours a day. I see the boy from the dream in front of me, and frantically tear at the stones to exorcise my terror and anger. It's dusk

THE EIGHTH HOUSE

now, and Justus calls and asks where I am. Breathless, I answer
that I'm headed home.

When I get home, Justus is already getting Vivi ready for bed.
I settle down on the sofa beside Sam. Every night Sam asks a
question that makes it too easy for me to choose Vivi.

'Who's going to do night-night with Vivi?' he asks.

I usually answer that I will, but this time I ask instead: 'What
do you want?'

'I think Dad should do night-night,' he says.

Now he leans towards me. I wrap my arm around him, and
he presses my hand to his chest. We sit like that in silence for
a while.

'I don't like it when they hit me at preschool,' he says finally.

I lean my head against his and close my eyes.

'Who hits you?'

'Hugo.' He blurts out the name accusingly. 'And Eino.'

I lift my head up from his and look at him. He won't meet
my eyes.

'They shouldn't do that,' I say. This isn't the first time we've
had this conversation. I choose my words carefully, but they
always end up the same, and I don't know if it's the right
thing to say. 'Do you tell an adult?'

'Yes.'

'What do the adults say?'

'They get mad at them. And tell us not to fight.'

And then? But I shut up. I don't know what more to do.
I wrap my arms around him.

'Have you ever hit anyone, Sam?'

I expect him to make that face he does when he says what
he thinks you want to hear, but today he doesn't. It seems
like he's really trying to remember.

'Yes, one time.'

'When was that?'

238

He thinks again, his gaze fixed somewhere in the distance.

'It was when I was 3,' he answers with a nod.

'Was it someone bigger, smaller or the same size as you?'

Sam grabs the fingers of one hand and stares down at them.

'Smaller,' he says quietly.

'How did that feel?'

When he answers, his voice is even softer.

'Not good,' he whispers.

I brush the hair out of his eyes. He needs a haircut.

'You know,' I tell him, 'Dad didn't learn fighting was bad until he was a lot older than you are now.'

He glances in my direction. I continue.

'He only learned when somebody hit his cousin really hard. After that, Dad never hit anyone again. It sounds like you learned the same thing when you were only 3. I think that's great.'

He leans into me, then snuggles into my arms. I stroke his back.

Every window in the Sommer house is open. Drawn curtains flutter like the white handkerchiefs of elegant women saying goodbye. At one end of the house, the sun is shining on a chequered tablecloth and wild flowers are displayed in vases. Sweat rolls off Ella Jonsson as she serves boiled haddock with egg sauce and fresh potatoes. Everyone around the table is talking past each other. Bumblebees buzz back and forth between the rose hips below the window and the bluebells on the dining table.

At the other, shadowy end of the house, spiders spin their webs undisturbed. The chatter of the Jonsson family penetrates the silence on the other side of the wall, where the Sommer family stay as far from each other as possible. The trial is over, but the interrogations continue. Bengt hasn't been convicted of anything in the eyes of the law; he's too young for that. But it doesn't matter. The Child Welfare Board has decided to take Bengt into protective custody, and the county administrative board confirmed their decision. He's being taken away from Perstorp, from his family, today. This time they don't know where, or to whom, he will be sent.

Otto, in a tank top, is lying on the kitchen sofa. The hum of his neighbours' happy family life seeping in annoys him. He grabs the back of the sofa and pulls himself up to a sitting position, walks into the dimly lit grey-blue living room. He turns on the radio. A glockenspiel is playing an awkward melody. He turns up the volume to drown out the Jonsson family, then lies back down on the sofa, folding his hands over his chest and closing his eyes. The melody ends, and the clock strikes slowly 12 times. Otto breathes to its rhythm. A voice announces that it's time for today's poem. A raspy voice full of emotion starts to read a poem by Einar Malm called 'Wraith'.

The street outside the Sommers' house is sticky with the sap of linden trees. Masses of bumblebees are scattered across the ground, all dead or dying. It always happens under the linden trees at this time of year, and nobody knows why. A rumble approaches and a black, glossy, beautifully curved car turns onto the street, rolling over the bumblebees. As the tyres make their way across the sap, they sound like something coming unstuck, tape being pulled free in one long motion. The sun shines on the silver hubcaps.

'Bengt,' Otto calls upstairs. 'They're here now.'

Three men get out of the car. Mr Ekvall, Parish Constable Gottfrid Andersson and a uniformed police officer. Bengt takes a step out onto the stairs with a suitcase in his hand. Behind Bengt, Otto stands grey-faced. The sound of a woman sobbing can be heard from inside the house.

'Who are you?' Otto says to the police officer.

The officer opens his mouth, but the parish constable answers instead.

'He's here from the Stockholm police.'

'Well. Are you taking him to Stockholm then?'

'Mr Sommer, you know we can't tell you where he's going,' Mr Ekvall answers, his expression regretful.

Otto's gaze moves over to him and lingers there. He saves his harshest judgment for Ekvall, because he's the only one who seems to feel the least bit guilty. And because he's known Bengt since he started school. Otto pats Bengt's shoulder, and Bengt falls against his chest, hiding his face there like a little boy. Otto's expression softens. He strokes the fragile spine of his son beneath his shirt and jacket, like a row of round stones beneath a blanket. His voice is thick when he speaks.

'We're gonna appeal.' He says it again, with his eyes fixed on Mr Ekvall, the representative of the Child Welfare Board. 'We will appeal this.'

'Of course, you have every right to do so,' the parish constable replies.

The police officer steps forward and grabs Bengt's elbow.

He pulls him out of his father's arms. Bengt's shoulders shake silently as he's led out to the car.

'Bengt!'

Rut calls his name over and over as the car rolls away over hundreds of bumblebees, while curious neighbours watch from behind their flowered curtains.

It's 7 May 2021 – on this day 73 years ago Birgitta died. I wake up with a sore arm. I got a tattoo yesterday. On my left arm, at elbow height, there are now three small flowers – lily of the valley, cotton-grass and blooming larch. After the tattoo artist drew the flowers, I asked if she had time to do one more. I've been thinking for a while that I'd like to have an S and a V somewhere, for Sam and Vivianne. 'Sure,' she replied. 'What do you want it to look like?' I hadn't thought much about it, but on a whim, I said I wanted there to be an eight in between them. 'Do you mean like the number eight or the eternity sign?' 'The eternity sign,' I replied. It was only as I was on my way home that I remembered the dream, when Birgitta told me to write an eight on a piece of paper and burn it with a sprig of lavender. I thought of the letter B, and of eternity, and it felt right.

Just like in 1948, 7 May falls on a Friday this year, I haven't been to Skogskyrkogården for a long time, I haven't felt up to seeing the graves. Lately I've felt like my insides have been covered by black plush, and I don't want to be reminded of death. But outside the cemetery wall there are larch trees growing. I want to see if they're in bloom.

Most of the other trees are still bare, or only budding. But as I approach the larch trees I can see they've already grown new, healthy green needles. And when I'm right beside them, I see the flowers. Small pink flowering cones. I jump up to grab on to one and pull it close. Raindrops lie like tiny jewels on raspberry-red pyramids. I break off a twig. It's soft and flexible. I jump even higher and grab another. The blackbirds are chirping above me in the branches.

Finally, I head home, heavy and sad. When I step into the elevator, I see myself in the mirror, ugly with tangled hair and the two twigs in my hand. I begin to cry before reaching our floor. When I open the door, I can hear Vivi speaking her incoherent baby language. Justus sees me.

'Oh, honey,' he says, 'what happened?'

I hold out the twigs to him and go to wash my hands. When I go out into the kitchen, Justus is reaching for one of the vases on top of the refrigerator. It's too big for those little twigs, but I'm touched because he knows I love that vase. He wraps his arms around me, and we stand like that for a long time. Until Vivi gets jealous and stretches her arms towards me. I let her put her sticky hands in my hair and on my best shirt, and she presses her mouth hard against mine.

I sit down at the computer and begin working, but only manage five minutes before the computer starts updating itself. The screen goes black. Suddenly, I'm crying again. I put my face in my hands, and the tears drip onto the desk. The wet spots look like milk on the reddish-brown wood.

I write a text message to Karl:

Thinking of Birgitta today, and of you, too.

He answers minutes later.

Hello Linda! Thank you! This morning my thoughts wandered to you but I hesitated to transmit them. But here they are. Hugs, Karl.

Senior Constable Gerell wakes up in a hotel room in Stockholm to a loudly ringing phone. His head is pounding. An almost empty glass stands on the small table in the corner, and a sweet aroma mingles with the dry, dusty smell of the carpet. It's hot and stuffy. The senior constable has to rub his eyes several times to wake himself up before he can figure out where the phone is. He sits on the bed and picks up the phone. A young woman's voice comes from the other end; it sounds like she's calling from the bottom of the sea.

'Good morning, Mr Gerell. A reporter from a news agency wishes to speak to you. Shall I connect him?'

He clears his throat loudly.

'Sure, go ahead.'

He glances at the clock – precisely eight in the morning. The phone clicks.

'Good morning, Senior Constable Gerell.' The reporter doesn't wait for answers, but heads straight to his questions. 'The head of the Swedish Board of Social Affairs Mr Eriksson, has spoken to *Dagens Nyheter* regarding the multiple interrogations of the Perstorp boy. Have you read it?'

'No. What did he say?'

'He says, *There must be no more of these endless interrogations of the boy. He's been questioned more than most criminals.* Do you agree with him? After all, it's been almost two months since the trial; surely this needs to end at some point.'

The senior constable laughs and stands up.

'That's funny, because the boy's only been questioned twice, once on the ninth of May and then on the twentieth of July.'

The reporter falls silent on the other end of the line. The senior constable can hear him leafing through his papers. Just as he starts to protest, a dumb-sounding 'Bu—', Gerell continues to speak.

'The fact is that I've wanted to break my silence and say my piece for long time. This case has been fully investigated from a criminal justice point of view. The boy *did* commit the crime.' Something races and buzzes inside his head. 'If he'd been tried as an adult, they would have put him away for a long time.'

'So you say,' replies the reporter, 'but those on the boy's side contend that the evidence never would have been sufficient for a conviction of an adult. They say that it's only because he's *not* of legal age that he was taken away from his home.'

Now Senior Constable Gerell can feel anger roaring through his body. He's so tired. His head is aching. He never wants to see Bengt again. He wants all this to be over. 'There's been way too much gossip and speculation!' he shouts, slashing his hand through the air, as if splitting a log. 'Yes, I've tried to speak to the boy, repeatedly. I've tried to give him a chance to ease his guilt. But he doesn't understand the right way, the only way! If he continues like this, the boy will be known as the Perstorp Youth for the rest of his life.'

He takes a deep breath, stands up and stares at himself in the mirror. His face is sweaty and swollen. A wisp of hair hangs down on his forehead, and he brushes it away.

'Do I understand this correctly? Are you, as a representative of the state prosecutor and the county board, claiming that the boy is guilty even though he hasn't been convicted?'

The journalist's question hangs in the air. Gerell is breathing heavily.

'You can be sanctioned for this,' continues the reporter.

'I don't give a f . . .' begins the senior constable. 'It's very possible. But I'll take my chances.'

The reporter's sharp pen can be heard rasping its quick and inharmonious dance across the paper.

'What you said about the interrogations. That there were only two. That may be the case as far as official police interrogations are concerned. But the boy *has been questioned* many, many times over, by different people, in different contexts. Mr Gerell, you, like Dr Sjödén, even visited the boy at his home, isn't that correct?'

The senior constable goes to the window next to the bed and opens it. Sounds and smells from the street below pour into the tiny room – garbage, asphalt, exhaust, a verdant lime tree. Cars, voices, a broom brushing against the pavement.

'It was a friendly visit. I just wanted to reason with the boy, help his parents understand our task.' He stares out at a clear sky. 'And as for the interrogations, as you like to call them, the boy has absolutely not been harmed by them. That's how tough he is.'

I find a letter in a filing cabinet. It's addressed to the lawyer Peyron and signed by Senior Constable Gerell on 14 July 1948. Peyron has asked to be present during the interrogation; he's been told that Gerell intends to detain Bengt later that day. Gerell says no. The trial is already over, but the interrogations, which Gerell insists are just talks and nothing else, continue. And there's no way there were only two interrogations. According to the surviving police records, Bengt had already been interrogated three times before he was taken to Ljungaskog on 10 or 11 May.

NEW LETTER FROM PERSTORP

The father of the Perstorp fourteen-year-old submitted another letter of complaint to the government, in which he, among other things, asks for consideration of the witness interviews held in Klippan from 6–7 of July.

The youth's father doesn't consider the results reached by the Danish National Police's technical department in their examination of the boy's shoes to be of any value and claims that the conclusions made after the examination 'are based on incomplete premises'. [. . .]

The father wants to hold the Child Welfare Board, acting Senior Constable Gerell and Dr Sjödén accountable. Much of what was expressed in the first letter is repeated here. Both letters of appeal are unclearly worded, and the arguments could be structured better. After reading both letters, one cannot help but wonder who wrote them. They certainly don't create the effect the father has intended, which is why he is to be pitied.

Otto Sommer slowly puts the newspaper down on the kitchen table and hides his face in his hands. He stays like that for a long time. The clock is ticking on the wall. The bumblebees are buzzing in the honeysuckle. It smells like burnt milk and coffee grounds. Otto pulls his feet together as if in a spasm, flexes his toes and releases them again, back and forth. Through his socks he can feel the texture of the rag rug. He shifts his weight from the kitchen chair to the floor as if to test if it's able to support him. With his back bent, his stomach contracting and his hands across his bony face, he stands still and silent for a long time.

In the seconds of silence that follow, I realise I'm there too. I stand with my legs wide as if to anchor myself to the wooden floor, hold my arms in tense arcs. With my eyes fixed on Otto, I tentatively lift my right foot and slowly lower it, from heel to toe. It creaks loudly and all of Otto's muscles tense. Mine too. My left foot is hanging in the air. I lower it beside my right. The floorboards squeak. This time Otto turns his head quickly in my direction. It scares me, but his gaze is unseeing, and I realise that he can't see me. I'm filled with sadness, horror, resignation and adrenaline, as Otto runs through me towards the front door. He throws it open and rushes outside. In the middle of the street, he stops and looks back, undecided, into his house where I stare at him, invisible.

Part Three
Bared Teeth

You cut down
the sick linden
to sow its evil
death

My trunk is ill
As all can see –
and should also
be taken down

But like a rare
lovely venom
another urge
consumes me

a dark desire
to birth

Eva Neander, 'Dead Idyll'

I first read the name Harriet Schelin on an autumn morning. I was lying in bed in our old apartment, and outside rusty red leaves swirled against a grey sky. There was a world out there that I wasn't a part of. Vivi wasn't born yet; like an extra organ she wallowed inside my stomach. Justus and Sam were just about to head to preschool and I could hear the shuffling of boots and overalls.

'Bye,' Justus said; Sam echoed him, more quietly.

I waved my hand and dropped it just as the door closed. Then I picked up my phone and googled Birgitta's name. The top image in the search was the photo from Birgitta's funeral, the one of the six white-clad girls carrying a coffin strewn with lilies of the valley. A little further down I saw another photo that I had first thought was taken at Birgitta's funeral, but from a different angle. Six little girls carrying a coffin. White dresses, socks and shoes. But when I looked closer, I could see that there were heavy, white lilies on the lid, not lilies of the valley. Another girl's body lay inside that coffin. Beneath the picture was her name – Harriet Schelin.

I started reading articles about Harriet in online newspaper archives and the records of the National Library, and I was shaken by how many similarities there were to Birgitta's case. Both girls were murdered in 1948. Both were subjected to blunt force to the head, probably with a stone in Birgitta's case, and definitely with a stone in Harriet's. Harriet was found at the GAIK football club clubhouse in Lundby on Hisingen in Gothenburg; the bloody stone was under the building. Thus, like Birgitta, Harriet was murdered near a football field. They were close in age – Birgitta was 9, Harriet 8. Approximately two months passed between the murder of Birgitta in northern Skåne and the murder of Harriet in western Gothenburg, and 220 kilometres separate the two scenes.

I read what the coroner said about Harriet's injuries. She was hit above the left eye, Birgitta in the left temple. Harriet's lip was bruised and blue on the left side. Birgitta had a cut in the same place, and the jawbone beneath was broken. Harriet had two deep gashes in the back of her head and an angular wound, which may have been the result of being pushed against a sharp corner. Birgitta's injury to the back of her head echoed in my mind.

However, there are two important points that distinguish the girls' cases from each other. First, someone was convicted of Harriet's murder. Arne Persson was a welder, born and raised in Lundby, and lived in his mother's house with his brother. In one article it is written that after many long interrogations he confessed, while elsewhere it's reported he retracted his confession. In court, Persson accused the police of putting words in his mouth and directing him in the reconstruction of the murder.

Second, Harriet was raped.

Birgitta's murder trial began at around the time Harriet was murdered, and articles about both cases appeared side by side in almost every newspaper. Was it just a coincidence that the cases were so similar? Are little girls usually murdered? I can find only a single article asking if the same perpetrator might be behind both murders. It's from the newspaper *Arbetet,* where on 6 July 1948, they wrote:

There is no shortage of voices claiming the brutal rape and murder in Gothenburg on Saturday night might have the same perpetrator as the Perstorp murder. Of course, no definitive conclusion to these theories

can be reached, and there's still little reason to assume that such a
connection exists.

I put the phone down and closed my eyes. It was dark. The bodies of two little girls lay motionless in the mud. Their faces turned to the right. What you could see of them was covered in pitch-black blood. Leaves and twigs were tangled in blonde hair. One girl's sock was rolled down. The other girl's dress was pulled up. I floated in the darkness and contemplated them. Suddenly they opened their eyes and stared straight into mine.

Saturday evening descends on a sulphur-yellow apartment building in Lundby, on the island of Hisingen in Gothenburg. It's four days until Bengt's trial begins in the Klippan courthouse. Behind a thin door with a weak lock, a man sits alone in the living room, exhausted from a long day's work. A woman and a little girl are in the kitchen. The Schelin family. It's a quarter to nine, there's thunder in the air and a radio programme is just ending when the little girl, Harriet, turns to her mother, Viola.

'Please, Mama, can I get some money for a hot dog?' says Harriet.

I try to imagine what it is she wants. Does she love hot dogs? Or does she just want not to be stuck at home? Is it a normal, childish longing for adventure, or is it something much sadder? Or maybe Harriet is just hungry; maybe she didn't have dinner.

'This late?'

Viola's youngest daughter tilts her head. Straight, blonde hair follows her movements like silk.

'Please, Mama, please.'

Viola considers it for a moment.

'You have to ask Papa for some change in that case.'

'Papa!' Harriet calls out immediately, turns and runs from the kitchen into the living room, which is also a bedroom.

It's dark in there. No one's turned on the lamp yet, and smoke hangs like a fog. Harriet's father's name is Johnny, and he comes from a long line of labourers. He sits slumped in an

257

armchair next to a small table with a radio on it. Harriet is handed two shiny 25-öre coins.

'Be home no later than nine thirty, Harriet,' Viola calls after her.

'I'll be home by nine thirty or ten,' she replies.

While Harriet is in the hall pulling on her sandals, her older sister, Irene, comes through the front door without knocking. She's 20 and has been married for a year, but still visits often. Irene says hello to her little sister and her father, before settling down at the kitchen table across from her mother.

'Is there any coffee?'

'Yes, there's a little left.'

'Bye,' Harriet calls as she heads through the door.

I start to panic now. It's so strange that they can't feel it too, this foreboding feeling that should make the hair on their arms stand up. Why aren't they moved to stop her, to tell her not to go out this late? I try to wrap my arms around her, but it's like hugging air.

Harriet goes out into the street and a cold wind pulls at her sandals. Then she sees the bus and runs to meet it. The driver greets her by name. There are no other children on the bus. She sits at the front and looks out the window. Every time she sees lightning, she jumps and counts the seconds until the thunder passes, working out in her head how far away the bolt struck.

'Three,' she says to the bus driver, 'three kilometres.'

'Well then, I think you should hurry home, Harriet,' he replies.

'Do you feel like a homicide detective?' my friend Anna asked me when we had a beer yesterday.

I let out a *ha*. 'No.'

'What *do* you feel like?'

I didn't think twice before answering: 'A mother.'

'To those girls?' she wondered.

Yes. And an instrument of vengeance.

I've been searching for someone with a deep knowledge of police work who can go through Birgitta's murder investigation with me. I want to hear an expert's thoughts. There's a glimmer of hope that the riddle of her death can be solved, if only I find the key. One morning I receive an email.

You didn't hear this from me, it says, *but look for the names of retired homicide detectives in old newspaper articles.* Two articles are attached, and I open the first one.

The police don't yet know if a crime lies behind the discovery of a human jaw at a waste processing plant in Saltsjö-Boo in Nacka.

The article appeared in *Svenska Dagbladet* on 5 July 2005. The reporter interviewed the head of the Nacka police's detective unit, Jan Ullén. The second article is from 11 March 2011.

31-year-old mother killed her newborn child and stored the body in her freezer − when she gave birth to the next child, she did the same.

Once again, Detective Superintendent Jan Ullén is answering questions about the case. I google his name, and all the headlines tell micro-stories of sudden, evil death. Perhaps I have found my man.

It is one o'clock in the morning, and Harriet's mother, father and sister are standing in the cone of light beneath a street lamp in the company of two police officers. The air is heavy, and there's a dull rumble on the horizon; the thunder is now moving away. The street lights cast yellow rings.

At ten thirty, when Harriet still hadn't come home, they'd gone down to the bus station. The hot dog stand is located just a few minutes away. It's not really necessary to take the bus, but Harriet likes riding it.

A bright voice rings out.

'Papa!'

They turn to see three boys running towards them. One stops in front of a police officer.

'What are you doing here?' the cop asks his son, who turns to his two friends.

'Tell them what you found.'

'There's a girl behind the clubhouse,' says one.

Johnny Schelin is already on his way. He runs so fast the torn fabric of his blue jacket flaps behind him, like wings. Just as he reaches the clubhouse, he skids on the gravel and falls. Crawling, he turns the corner, and collapses beside what was once his daughter.

I'm trying to find a phone number for Jan Ullén; there are seven people by that name in Sweden. I'm nervous and it's Sunday evening by the time I finally muster up the courage to send a text message to the most likely candidate.

Hi Jan! I'm researching a cold murder case. Are you the Jan Ullén who was a detective at the Nacka police? Would you consider talking to me?

He answers quickly.

Yes, I'm that Jan. You're welcome to call me tomorrow. You have my phone number.

It takes forever to get Vivi to sleep that evening. When I finally dare to move away from her, she follows, reaching for me. Finding only a pillow, she pulls her arms back and embraces herself in sleep. I head out and sit down at my computer. I have to formulate my questions for Jan Ullén. I wonder if Birgitta's case is familiar to all homicide detectives, or if it's been long forgotten.

What I most want to ask Jan is if he thinks the investigation had been properly conducted, if it seems reasonable to consider Bengt the culprit, and how such a police investigation would have gone today. Does he too see the similarities between the murders of Birgitta and Harriet? Are multiple blows by a rock to the back of a girl's head, temple and jaw something unique, or just part of a pattern, a tapestry of common, run-of-the-mill murders?

After breakfast the next day, I extricate myself from my family at the kitchen table and head to the study. My nervousness quickly drains out of me when I hear Jan's voice, which is friendly and confident. He'd like to help, and asks me to send him the investigation. 'It's always exciting, helping with these historic cases,' he says.

After I send him a zipped file, I head towards Skogskyrkogården. I'm waging a silent war with the cemetery administration. I keep planting flowers on my grandfather's, grandmother's and aunt's shared grave, and the groundskeepers keep pulling them out. I don't know why, and I haven't asked. Vivi has fallen asleep in her pushchair with the cat in her hand. With no wadding left in its neck, its head hangs and flops. It's starting to resemble a wrung-out dishcloth.

When I'm almost home again, I get an email. It's from Jan. *Hey, I'm reading now. I'll be in touch soon. Jan.*

It's a cold Friday. I'm reviewing Birgitta's and Harriet's cases in my head. They're too similar to be coincidental. And if it's the same perpetrator, Bengt couldn't possibly be the culprit. He couldn't have gone to Gothenburg just before the trial. The more I think about it, the more certain I become. It had to be the same person who murdered them both. And it wasn't Bengt. Who, then? Could Arne Persson, the welder convicted of Harriet's murder, have done it?

I go upstairs to call Karl.

'Hello,' he replies after just one ring.

'Hello, Karl, it's Linda.'

I know Karl's parents believed Bengt was responsible for their daughter's murder, and I think Karl too found a kind of solace in that conclusion. But now I'm about to hint that I'm not sure it was Bengt. That it could have been someone else. I've been afraid to talk to Karl about this, I don't want to disturb his peace of mind.

To my immense relief, Karl doesn't mind when I tell him my doubts. It sounds as though this is a new possibility to him, one he hasn't considered before.

We start wrapping up our conversation. He's pleased that I am writing and says I should work on the story in whatever way I choose. I ask him to tell his sister Eva, who has decided not to discuss the past with me, that her real name won't appear in whatever final form my writing on the case takes, whether that be a book or otherwise. But we don't hang up.

I decide to tell him something I've never mentioned before, for fear he might be shocked: that sometimes it feels like Birgitta is helping me along, that she wants to tell her story through me.

'That almost sounds a little . . . Christian,' says Karl.

I laugh.

'Or, maybe, what do they call it . . .' he continues.

'Spiritual?' I suggest.

'Yes, spiritual,' says Karl.

'You're not very spiritual?'

'No, I wouldn't say so.'

There's a rustle at the other end of the line.

'What do you think happens after we die?' I say.

It's an enormous question to ask someone. But it just flew out of my mouth. Karl is silent for a while.

'Well. I think it is probably a blackness.'

'Do you really believe that?'

'I hope that's not the case.' He pauses. 'I hope I'll see Mama and Papa again.'

I go to bed with the two murders swirling inside my mind. When I finally fall asleep, I dream of a man hitting me in the head, and do my best to defend myself. I wake up with a terrible pain at the back of my head. It's a new feeling. Is this a migraine? I can't move, can barely breathe. Justus is sleeping just behind me, but I can't turn over. Instead, I pick up the phone and call him. He replies with a confused 'Hello?'

'Help,' I whisper, 'it hurts so much.'

He gets up to look for something that might help, anything. While he's gone, the pain worsens. It takes him a thousand years. I consider calling an ambulance; it feels like I'm dying. It must be serious if it hurts this much. My face has turned to stone. Justus arrives with some painkillers and a glass of water.

'Okay, well, goodnight. Hope it gets better soon,' he says.

'Bye,' I whisper.

Bye? Why did I say that? Justus clambers back into bed and soon he's snoring. The pain slowly slips away. At three o'clock Vivi wakes up, and I crawl in next to her. It takes forever to calm her down. When she wakes up again at six in the morning, my arm beneath her head is numb like a broken wing.

The rain patters against the window, and a draught flows from the door while I eat my breakfast sandwich in front of the computer. My coffee's been cold a long time. I drain the last of it. Then I call Jan Ullén.

He starts out by saying he thinks the police investigation in Perstorp was good overall, especially considering it was

1948. I respond 'Ah, okay,' a little disappointed. He, if anyone, would know.

'But there are some loose ends I would have looked into, and which I can't find any documentation for in the police investigation. There's this man in the swimming trunks, or shorts, who was seen in the clearing.'

'Right! The one Elin Sjöberg saw,' I exclaim.

'Yep, she observed the man, and also reacted strongly to the dog barking at the forest. The police write they conducted an investigation, but it's not clear what that consisted of.'

No. The records state that there were often sportsmen up in that forest. If any of them were interrogated, those interrogations were weeded out. I've often wondered why one of them would take off all of his clothes besides his underpants.

'What's a bit strange about Bengt is that in the first inter-rogation he says he went straight home. And then when he's confronted by Edvin Oskarsson, he changes his statement.'

'I've thought a lot about that,' I say, 'how Bengt changes his story after his football coach talks to him in private.'

'Yes,' says Jan. 'This Edvin Oskarsson. I'm quite curious about him.'

I sigh silently, releasing long-held tension. I've wondered if my suspicion towards Oskarsson was just wishful thinking on my part – casting doubt on an adult because I find it so hard to imagine the killer being a child.

'And nobody sees Oskarsson wash his hands,' continues Jan. 'That's a bit odd, too. No, I would have looked at Oskarsson more closely.'

Just like when I went to Lund to read the police report two years ago, I've left the tree buds behind in Stockholm and have been greeted by blooming lilacs. Down here in Perstorp it's already early summer.

After Justus got his licence, the first thing I did was plan another road trip back here, with him as driver. Perstorp has put its best foot forward today – green and warm. I open the car window and breathe it in, straighten up and pull my pony-tail tight. We drive through downtown, headed towards the football field. Today I'm going to time exactly how long Bengt's and Edvin's routes would have taken. We've decided I'll go alone; everything takes so much longer with a baby.

'Ugh, I'm nervous,' I say, suddenly feeling too hot.

'It'll be fine,' Justus says, looking into my eyes before bending his head over his phone.

I suddenly remember how much I wanted him to put his hand on my belly to feel the baby kick. How I wanted him to be as fascinated by it as I was.

'See you later,' I say after a few seconds, and close the car door.

The path Bengt said he took from the football field to the dump no longer exists. I try to walk as close to where it lay as possible. It's not easy. The forest has become inhospitable. It doesn't want me here. Almost immediately I stumble across larch trees. Large, powerful and old larch trees. Surely these were the ones the teacher was referring to when she told Birgitta they were growing above the football field? Birgitta probably never had time to find them. If she had, a bouquet of larch flowers surely would have been found near the crime scene. I lay my hand on their bark, turn my face upwards and close my eyes.

I don't get far into the forest before I'm forced to go back to the footpath that winds between the dense trees. As it thins out a bit, I try to follow the old road again, but I'm met by a sign warning there's a shooting range ahead. I back away again. Soon I'll arrive at the lake. The last part of the road that once led to the dump lies beneath water today. It's taken me about twelve and a half minutes to walk here. When the police asked Bengt how long it took, he said: 'Maybe five minutes. I walked a little, ran a little.'

I head back in the direction of the football field, then turn left towards the site where the Sommers' house once stood. It's been torn down, as has the house next to it. Nobody's built anything new here. It's just two square lots of swaying grass and dandelions. The neighbourhood surrounding them seems odd. Half the houses are freshly painted, robot lawn-mowers roll around in front of them, and the cars parked outside are shiny. The other half have boarded-up windows and flaking paint.

In 1948, when the police timed the route between the new football field and Bengt's house, it took six minutes; for me the same distance took more than twice as long. But the path I took was shaped like an upside-down L — Bengt must have cut straight between the two points, which isn't possible today.

I head towards the downtown area. On the way I pass by a large field of lilies of the valley. No flowers yet, just little green buds. I stop and look. When I'm about to start walking again, I glance at the ground in front of me and notice I'm about to step on a dead baby bird. It's completely flat, as if several people have already done so. I stop, my foot still in the air, and take a long step over it.

On my way to the neighbourhood where Edvin Oskarsson once lived, I walk along Köpmangatan, where Café Centrum was located. Edvin said that he went there for about fifteen minutes after meeting with Assar Andersson.

Elin Sjöberg's farm was located below a building that now houses a plastics museum. I imagine a scenario where Edvin is the man Elin Sjöberg saw, and realise that he couldn't have gone home to get dressed. It's too far between the Sjöberg farm and Edvin's place, and regardless of whether he walked through the garden or along the street, someone would have noticed a half-naked man. By chance, I happen to pass by what used to be the Sivander family home. New people live here now. I freeze when I recognise where I am. Standing on the sidewalk, I look sideways so no one will realise I'm staring.

The road to Elin Sjöberg's farm still exists, but it leads nowhere. The grass on either side is so tall you see nothing but swaying blades and sky. Soon I arrive where the farm used to be. It's more sparsely overgrown here. It only took me five minutes to walk over from Birgitta's house. I close my eyes and see Birgitta in front of me, the St Bernard dog's big paws in her hands; they're dancing, the dog howling with joy. A stream runs opposite where the farm once stood. On the other side of the stream sits the forest where Elin saw the man appear and walk in the direction of the football field.

I head towards the stream. It's thick with vegetation and difficult to reach, but then another field of lilies of the valley opens up. A few are already in bloom. Could this have been Birgitta's secret lily-of-the-valley source, where the flowers bloomed long before anywhere else? I get down on all fours and poke my nose into the white bells, breathing their pure scent deep into my lungs. Just then I hear steps on the road and glance over my shoulder. It's a man. He has a long, narrow case slung over his shoulder; perhaps he is headed to the shooting range? My face turns red from embarrassment as I stand up and brush off my clothes.

'Hello there,' I say.

'Hey,' he answers, nodding, a neutral expression on his face.

I wait until I can't see him anymore before turning back towards the forest. I try to move forward, but I can't. It's too densely overgrown. I turn around and head back towards the football field.

It takes no more than five minutes. I'm surprised the distance is so short; it felt longer when Mimmi and I drove it. I take out the maps and study them closely. It's getting close to Vivi's dinner time, and it takes half an hour to drive to Munka-Ljungby, where we're staying tonight. I jog towards the site of the murder, pushing branches and scrub to the sides. There it is, that dark ditch. I stare down the moss-covered banks into the brown water below. So many birch leaves. I sink down into a crouch. Without thinking, I press my hand to my left temple. It aches intensely, throbbing and pulsing. I close my eyes and the image of Birgitta on the autopsy table flashes before me.

Suddenly Justus is calling.

'Hello?' I answer.

'Hey, listen, don't freak out, but there are two security guards headed your way.'

I go cold.

'What?'

'Yes, they came by here asking me why we'd been parked for so long. And apparently, they saw you on a surveillance camera.' He laughs, and I can hear Vivi whimpering in the background. 'They think you're here for industrial espionage or something.'

At that very second, a car pulls over on the road. The doors fly open and two men in uniform stare me down. I smile and say I know how strange all this must have looked on the surveillance camera, but I cross my heart and promise I'm not spying on the nearby factory. 'What are you up to then?' they ask. I tell them that I'm researching an old murder case, and point down into the ditch. 'This is where the murder happened.' They haven't heard about any murder and are curious for details. I don't give them much.

'Is it haunted?' asks one.

I let out a forced laugh.

'I don't think so,' I say.

They climb into their car, after joking that they'll have their eyes on me. I grin and wave. Then I let my smile fall.

Before we leave Perstorp, we pass by a grocery store. I buy a grave candle and a bouquet of red roses, while Justus and Vivi wait in the car. Then we drive the short distance to Perstorp's church. It's started raining heavily, and we hurry into the cemetery. I light the candle and place it on the red stone, then put the roses beneath Birgitta's name.

That evening, I put Vivi to sleep while Justus takes a sauna and a swim downstairs. Afterwards, I settle into an armchair by the large window that looks over the pond and jetty where they used to wash and pound laundry in the olden days. From where I'm sitting, I can see the paddocks, too, and the forest behind. As darkness falls, huge shadows start streaming out of the forest. Wild boar.

'Your turn,' says Justus as he comes out wrapped in a towel and bathrobe.

While I'm in the sauna, I think about how difficult it was to get to the forest above the football field.

'Wild', the chairman called it in court. I cross my legs. At certain points, thorns penetrated my jeans and scratched the skin. Why would anyone want to wander around in nothing but shorts there? I'm trying to piece together the various lengths of time it took me to walk between points. But it all spins together in my head. I need to make sense of it out loud, so I step out of the sauna and climb into cold water.

'Okay, it's like this,' I begin and Justus looks up. 'I imagine the person who murdered Birgitta saw her at the edge of the forest. He approached her and asked what she was doing there

272

alone. She didn't usually talk to strangers, her father said, so it was either someone she knew, or someone she trusted. Maybe he said, "I work with your father," or "I know your brother." And when he asked her what she was doing, she told him, "I'm looking for larch trees." "Oh, yeah," he replied, "I know where the larch trees are."

'Then he takes her with him. He tries to get her to undress. Takes off her shoes and starts to remove her socks, but she resists. He hits her. She gets scared and starts to run. He's afraid she'll tell someone what he's done. He catches up to her, hitting her several times in the back of the head, turns her around and hits her in the temple. Then he picks up all those rocks and the half-rotten stump and places them on top of her. By then he'd be pretty dirty, right? Not just bloody, but muddy, covered in old leaves, moss, pine needles etc.'

'Uh-huh.'

'He walks further up into the forest and takes off his clothes. He buries them together with the murder weapon. And then he goes down from the forest in the opposite direction, towards Elin Sjöberg's farm. There are far fewer people on that side. But Elin happens to see him.'

'Okay?'

'It took about five minutes to walk from the new football field to the site of the murder. From the clearing where Elin Sjöberg saw the man, it takes just as long to return to the new football field. He went to the changing room and washed off. There was a box of clean clothes for the football team, the ones Edvin had gone to check on. Surely there was at least one pair of trousers left behind too. He got dressed and rode his bike or walked away.'

'Yes, that sounds reasonable,' says Justus. He's silent a moment and looks out towards the forest before continuing. 'You've completely written off Bengt, haven't you?'

'No.' Justus hands me a beer; I take a sip and think a bit. 'Not really, it took him a very long time to get home. If he left the football field shortly after 7:30 say 7:35, and according to his account it took five minutes to get to the dump, because he half ran to make it before dark . . . And then five minutes back. According to the police, it took six minutes to walk from there to Bengt's home. He came home between 8:12 and 8:15.' I count in a whisper. 'So he has around twenty minutes unaccounted for. It sounds like he basically got to the dump and turned around again. So what did he do with those extra twenty minutes? It could also be as simple as the fact that he was 14 years old and didn't have a very good sense of time. I mean, I would have a very hard time explaining what I did yesterday and how long everything took, and I'm an adult. Maybe he left the football field later than he thought, or maybe it took him longer to get to the dump than five minutes. That seems reasonable.'

'Hmm,' replies Justus.

I climb out of the pool and go back into the sauna. I'm trying to calculate how much time Edvin might have had, but that's more difficult. He said he biked to Assar Andersson at about a quarter to eight, and that cycling there would have taken about ten minutes. Assar said he arrived at half past seven. But that can't be true, as at that time he was supposed to still be at the football field. Before a quarter past eight, he biked from Assar's to Café Centrum. He stayed there for about fifteen minutes before biking home. Elin said she witnessed the man at about a quarter to eight. It was as the sun dipped down behind the treetops. She saw him in the last rays of sunshine. I step out of the sauna, shower and pull on a bathrobe. Then I go out to my phone and search 'Perstorp sunset May 7 1948'. On that evening it set at 7:58.

If the man seen by Elin was the murderer, and if the assumption that Birgitta was murdered around seven thirty is correct, the perpetrator would have had about a quarter of an hour. Is it possible to attack a girl, kill her, lift heavy stones and a stump out of the ground and cover her body with them, take off your clothes, hide them and get down to the clearing in that amount of time? I don't know. It doesn't sound like a long time, but if you're pumped full of adrenaline, maybe it's possible. Could Edvin have had time to kill Birgitta before heading to Assar? Come down from the forest in just shorts, snuck into the changing room and put on new clothes before riding his bike away? The football field, the murder site and Elin's farm are all very close to each other, but it still doesn't sound likely. What if Edvin was never actually at Assar's? No, if they'd colluded there wouldn't have been inconsistencies between the times. Could it have been someone else completely?

Given how uncertain the timing was, the time span could be extended. Perhaps Birgitta had already been attacked at 7:25. Maybe Elin was wrong by five minutes. That would give the perpetrator 25 minutes. And that's not unreasonable. But it still tells us nothing. Who was it? Who? Who? I lie down next to Vivi in the dark, soundlessly thinking *Please* over and over, and *Show me who it was*. But when I wake up the next morning my memory is as blank as a windless lake.

Lately I've spent a lot of time trying to find other violent crimes that took place near Perstorp around the time of Birgitta's murder. I find it hard to believe that this was someone's first or last act of violence. Surely a person doesn't just wake up one day and like a bolt out of the blue decide to kill another person, strike a little girl repeatedly in the head with a rock, cover her body and then go on to lead a normal life? I find more than a few unpleasant cases in and around Perstorp. I write to Mimmi about it and she replies: *Beloved Perstorp. Our portal to the underworld.*

That sums up my feelings exactly. The murder and the town have become mythological in my mind. Birgitta plays the role of a fairy-tale princess, a Princess Tuvstarr. Tuvstarr's crown was stolen by the elves, her dress by the forest witch, and finally her golden heart was taken by the deep pond in the woods. Naked and alone, the little girl was left looking into the dark water forever after.

In my mind the evil forest is almost an extension of Perstorp. But I've sensed that the mood in the Perstorp Facebook group has changed lately. It feels lighter and more pleasant these days. The latest post is from a woman who lost one of her Ecco sandals. It's been shared 13 times. That's surely an act of good-will. Then there are the beautiful pictures of nature, reports of fox sightings in the area, folks wishing each other a great weekend, and old black and white pictures of people standing in front of farms and houses that no longer exist. It's clear that people look back fondly on their childhood in Perstorp, and many families have been there for generations. But in my heart Perstorp remains the dark backdrop to an evil drama.

There are several Princess Tuvstarrs in or near Perstorp over the years, girls and women unwillingly cast in different retellings of the story. Two of them are attacked within a few years of Birgitta's murder. In November 1948, a 17-year-old girl is handed the crown. She's cycling home from a dance late at night when a man runs down from the woods and knocks her off her bike. He drags her a few hundred metres into the forest. What he does to her in there I don't really know, but she survives and manages to escape. The police don't consider her credible, and the case is closed.

In January 1952, the imaginary crown is placed on the head of woman who was then exactly the same age as I am now. She too was on her way home from a party. The weather had changed during the evening, and her bicycle tyres were slipping on the icy road that runs through the forest east of Perstorp, the same vast forest in which Birgitta was found. The woman stops and lays the bike on the side of the road. Then a man comes rushing out of the black spruces, towards her. He rapes her and cuts her hands with a knife. Afterwards, he leaves her, bleeding, to her fate. The woman manages to drag herself to a neighbouring farm, where they patch her up. There was a blizzard after that, and only in the morning were they able to reach the police and call for a doctor. The woman recognised the man, but didn't know his name. The police pieced together who it was from her description, a man by the name of Hilding, and arrested him later that evening.

I search for 'rape' in the Perstorp group and find a post that reads: *Our local celebrity had something on his conscience.* There's an old article attached about this incident. The rest of the evening I read post after post about local celebrity Hilding Samuelsson. He was 19 when he was sentenced to six years of penal service for rape. I learn he had a difficult childhood and that he grew up in an orphanage, subjected to physical abuse and isolation. Once, when he was 12, he tried to break through the door of his isolation cell. He was often forced to stay there for three days in a row. Sometimes he'd have outbursts of rage and went 'berserk', it says. There's a picture of him as a young man dressed in a sailor suit, but in most pictures, he's older with long, unkempt hair and a beard. Until his death in the 1990s he played the role of Perstorp's village idiot. Everyone knew him, and judging by the Facebook posts – all from men – he was well liked. Almost all the comments under the posts about him were positive, even nostalgic. On closer inspection, I find a few outliers, a number of now grown women who describe how afraid they were of Hilding as little girls, but their concerns are downplayed. Several report that Hilding gave them a coin or a piece of candy, which made them more favourably disposed towards him.

Maybe they instinctively sensed something was off. I'm reminded of Urban. He worked at the same factory as me one summer and stared at me all the time. I tried to avoid him, but one day he found me alone in the staff room and cornered me. I don't remember much about the incident, only how trapped and afraid I felt. My boss promised to take it seriously, and when I asked him a few days later if he'd spoken to Urban, he told me he had. But then he explained that Urban was a special person, that his life hadn't been easy, and suggested Urban and I get a coffee together, just the two of us. I left and never went back again.

When Birgitta was murdered, Hilding Samuelsson was 15, about to turn 16. Unlike Bengt and Edvin, he had a history of violence, both receiving and committing it. 'The best indicator of future violence is past violence,' writes the criminal profiler John E. Douglas. I send a text message to Karl: *Do you remember a kid named Hilding? He was 2–3 years older than you. Lived in Perstorp with his mother and spent a few years in an orphanage.*

The answer arrives quickly. He remembers no Hilding.

At 8 or 9 years old, you're a whole person. You have dreams, favourite clothes, your own interests. There are things you hate, sometimes even people. There are things you love. Your feelings are as intense as any adult's. I was 8 when one autumn day I chose my own clothes for school. I've never felt more beautiful. Ribbed olive-green cotton tights, a wide-collared fleece jumper with a zigzag pattern in that same green, soft red and off-white. Added to that was a French braid. I had a best friend, fell in love for the first time and listened to my favourite song over and over. I knew every word by heart. That girl is still inside me; she expanded and became who I am today.

I can't find much to tell me about Birgitta and Harriet as people. I see them as still existing, but no one else does. When I ask Karl about what Birgitta was like as a person, his answers are evasive. I don't know if it's because he doesn't remember or because it's too hard for him to talk about it. But I receive tiny glimpses through newspaper articles and interrogations.

When we talked, I asked Jan Ullén if he knew anyone else who could help me with Birgitta's case, and he gave me a name. The person had been working with the police for close to half a century and has solid experience in criminal profiling. Later he'll tell me he wants to remain anonymous. We agree I'll refer to him as the Detective Inspector and not go into any detail about his actual duties.

I notice that he's cautious and a little sceptical of me. He wants to be sure that my intentions are good. I explain what

I'm doing, and after a long conversation he gets onboard. When I express my gratitude to him – 'thousands and thousands of thank yous' – he laughs loud and heartily. I send him Birgitta's police investigation, and he agrees to draw up a perpetrator profile based on it. He'll be doing this in his spare time so it might take a while. The day after our conversation, he sends me a message. He asks me to tell him what I know about Birgitta as a person, and I answer:

Birgitta used to jog with her father on the track at the football field. She was fast, good at tag. Most of her friends were boys, but not older boys. Her biggest interest was flowers. She liked picking them alone. Once she made the mistake of telling two other girls about a field of lilies of the valley and they told others. That made her angry, and after that she went only by herself. She knew the area well, but her father didn't think she would go by herself as high up into the forest as where she and her shoes were found. According to her father, she was high-spirited, and very friendly with those she'd met before, but would not have gone with someone she didn't know. Earlier that day, she'd been at home with a stomach-ache. Maybe just to avoid school.

In the morning, I head to the National Library. I take the elevator down to the basement and pull open the heavy door to the Microfilm Reading Room. It hasn't shut behind me before I'm already in front of one of the screens.

Harriet Schelin's body is still warm when it's found behind the clubhouse in Lundby. So they carry her to the police car and drive at full speed to the children's hospital. But once there, the doctors can only confirm that she's dead.

In two newspapers there's a picture of Harriet smiling. She's almost straight-mouthed, with just the corners turned up. Her gaze is directed upwards and to the right, one eyebrow is raised, like an old vaudeville performer. Her hair is cut to her earlobes, and there's a comically large, dark bow sitting in her bangs. It looks like she knows how funny it looks. I read in the articles that she collected coins and amused herself by trading them with tram drivers, first swapping them for bills, then swapping them back for coins of various denominations, and then into bills again. She was also a gifted musician, playing both accordion and harmonica. Harriet was good friends with a Mrs Sofia Johansson, whom the newspapers interviewed.

It will feel so empty around here without her and that accordion, she said.

They'd met in the late morning on the day she was murdered. They discussed Mrs Johansson turning 75 the next day.

Harriet was so happy about it, she was going to come to my place early on the morning of my birthday and play me the most beautiful song we knew, "The Lily of the Valley's Farewell".

They headed out into the yard, and Harriet practised playing it for the other children.

Oh, how I longed to spread my scent to all,
praise my benevolent creator
with whatever scent I have left.
My short time will soon be over
and I bow my head so slow, so slow
to die, white as snow,
slumbering stilly into peace.

I've just gone to bed when an email arrives from the Detective Inspector. He's finished his criminal profile. My sleeping pill just kicked in, and I can barely keep my eyes open, but still skim through the six-page document. At the end, there's a summary. A young man, 15 to 20 years of age, actual or mental age. He was sexually inexperienced. He might have committed previous crimes, such as sexual attacks or violent assault. He was in good physical shape, despite his difficulty in catching up to Birgitta, who managed to get 60 metres through the forest before being caught in the ditch. He lived in Perstorp or had connections there. The Detective Inspector bases this on the fact that the perpetrator tried to hide Birgitta's body by submerging it in water. A person with no connection to Perstorp would have just left her there.

He was probably familiar with Birgitta, maybe only super-ficially. He had difficulty handling conflict and setbacks, and could become aggressive when they arose, due to limited impulse control. This profile doesn't match Edvin. I've thought some of the circumstantial evidence pointed towards him as the perpetrator, so find myself a little disappointed. It could be Bengt, except for one key point: the violence. The boys in Bengt's class agreed that Bengt, despite being the strongest one in the class, was nice. Then again, there was Barbro, the girl on the ice, who testified in court. Britta and Anita, the girls who Bengt asked if they wanted to 'go to the woods and screw', as well. The three girls had found Bengt unpleasant, and I understand why. The question is whether he himself was

283

aware of it. What was a 14-year-old boy taught to think appropriate at that time? To my ears, the events the girls brought up in court sound like something that might have happened without any predatory motives.

And then we have the incident that took place several years earlier, when Bengt was 8 years old. When in anger he picked up a piece of a scythe from the ground and threw it at his friend's older brother. How much can we read into that? At that age, you don't have much sense of consequences. Couldn't any 8-year-old have done the same? A boy, anyway. Boys are taught that a certain level of violence is acceptable. I read the summary of the criminal profile again and have another thought: aren't many of these elements a good fit for Hilding Samuelsson?

It was raw and damp, and the ground smelled like fungus and mould on the November day in 1938 when Senior Constable Gerell, accompanied by two men from the Child Welfare Board, knocked on the door of a cottage on the outskirts of Perstorp. It was little more than a shack, and a single mother was living there with her children. The senior constable had come to take them away. Not because of domestic violence, but because the home was so poor it was deemed unsuitable. One of the children was a 6-year-old boy. He tried to hide under his mother's skirts. The boy's name was Hilding, and he could hear his mother screaming his and his siblings' names as he was taken away to a foster home 70 kilometres away.

Hilding's social services records arrive in the mail in a thick brown envelope. I sit on the floor in the living room and follow him from orphanage, to foster home, to institution, while Justus puts Vivi to bed upstairs, and Sam plays with his Lego. Hilding bounced from one place to the next. Nobody wanted him. According to the records, he got into fights, ate horse manure and started fires. Assuming this is true, it describes a child who is deeply unwell. The employees at these homes, the people who were supposed to be helping Hilding, repeat the same words to describe him: 'unreliable', 'abnormal' and, above all, 'psychopath'. I wonder what the meaning of that word was at the time. In an article on alcoholism in a newspaper from 13 September 1933, psychopathy is defined as a 'mild mental abnormality'. I read several articles containing the word 'psychopathy' from around the time of Hilding's care, and they all seem to use it to mean an 'abnormal personality'. Not quite the definition we use today. But it's clear that many who came into contact with Hilding over the years found him unpleasant. They couldn't handle him. How would he have been seen today? What kind of help would he have received?

In the spring semester of 1946, Hilding's teacher describes how he would act when someone did something he didn't like. No matter if it was an adult or child, he would find them in the dining room, fix his eyes on his target and walk over to them. Then he'd start circling slowly around that person, repeating an abusive sentence, over and over, until his victim would break down and start to cry. The teacher herself had been subjected to it. 'Fucking nasty bitch,' was what he muttered to her. He was no stranger to physical violence either. Several incidents are described, directed at children and adults, women as well as men.

When Hilding Samuelsson was 8, he was placed in Råby's Home for Psychopathic Children in Lund. It was in the cold winter of 1941. Five years earlier, Råby had come under fire when a journalist named Else Kleen accused its director, Oskar Ekelin, of pure sadism. Kleen wrote of how these reformatory schools often, through their cruelty, turned harmless idiots into vicious young men.

At the time Hilding was placed at Råby, Ekelin was still the director. After two months, Hilding started to experience bouts of pain in his abdomen and blood appeared in his stool, so he was sent to a hospital in Kristianstad. His medical records state:

According to chief physician Dr Selander, his behaviour here was that of a pronounced psychopath, sometimes obstinate, sometimes surly, reluctant, depressed, he had attacks of pain in the abdomen together with severe vomiting, especially when upset or if something went against him. These attacks could last for several days, were amenable to psychotherapy, simpler forms of medication, etc. Intelligence: 10–11 years old.

Why was Hilding receiving psychotherapy? After all, he wasn't admitted for any mental illness, so why did the chief doctor provide a statement about Hilding? Was it Råby who requested it? It seems like Dr Selander suspected that Hilding's stomach pain sprang from psychological causes. I don't know how he explained the blood in the stool. And there it is again, the most common word in the record journals to describe Hilding over the years: 'psychopath'. What does it mean to call an 8-year-old a psychopath? I wonder what was written in other children's records at that time.

When Hilding is discharged from Råby, he's sent first to a foster home, but after only five months they refuse to keep him there. He's transferred to the Trelleborg orphanage. On his way to school, he collects empty bottles for returns. Using the money, he buys matches and lights fires, both at the orphanage and in the town of Trelleborg. He starts breaking windows and furniture. Something's happened. I think of the blood in the stool. And of how children, when they have anxiety, often describe this as a stomach-ache. Could he have been molested, or am I reading too much into it?

After seven months at the orphanage, Hilding is sent back to Råby. Two years later, he's admitted again with abdominal pain, but no diagnosis can be made. He continues to set fires. By the summer of 1946, Hilding has become so violent towards his peers and the adults at Råby that they consider him too dangerous to keep there. They request he transfer to the Lövsta Reformatory near Vagnhärad, almost five hundred kilometres north of Perstorp. That's where the worst boys end up, and it's also the institution Dr Birger Sjödén directs – the doctor who repeatedly had conversations with Bengt during the investigation into Birgitta's murder.

I had expected that everything would get ten times worse at Lövsta, but Hilding's grades get better, and he's described in more positive terms. In November 1947, he's discharged conditionally to his home in Perstorp. At this point, it's exactly nine years since he was taken away. Another familiar name appears as Hilding's probation officer – the teacher and Child Welfare Board member Sven Ekvall. Ekvall helps Hilding find a job at a butchery, but he doesn't like it. Then he starts working for his uncle, a trencher. He's described as willing and diligent, and works evenings without being asked. In March 1948, he quits and takes a few odd jobs here and there, before starting work as a hired hand for a farmer. Things seem to be going okay; *His employers, neighbours, and even his mother have expressed their full satisfaction with Hilding's behaviour,* writes Ekvall. Hilding uses his savings to buy a suit and a bicycle.

In May, Birgitta is murdered. Three names in Hilding's records are recognisable from the murder investigation: Senior Constable Gerell, Dr Sjödén and Sven Ekvall. None of them seems to point any suspicion in the direction of Hilding, a 15-year-old with a documented history of violence, who lived in Perstorp at the time of the murder. Why is that? Did they know for sure that Hilding couldn't have been on the scene? I wonder whether it might have had something to do with Perstorp as a place. Karl has told me how class divisions characterised the town, the biggest difference being between salaried employees and factory workers. His family belonged to the first group, the Sommer family to the second. Hilding's family were a notch below the Sommer family economically. They were poorer than the working families, so poor that Hilding and his siblings weren't allowed to live with their mother. But their roots ran deep and strong in the soil of Perstorp. Bengt, on the other hand, was half German. He stood with one foot among the working classes, the other among refugees. And the refugees were the true others, the town's real outsiders. Through his father, he was connected to the foreigners in the factory barracks. The foreigners Otto Sommer was asked about during the trial. Perhaps it was out of loyalty to their own group, to the Swedes and the people of Perstorp, that Senior Constable Gerell, Dr Sjödén and Ekvall never considered Hilding?

A month and a half after Birgitta is murdered, Hilding goes to the Lövsta Reformatory for a visit and stays for six days. It's not clear why, but it seems strange that he would go there as a 'holiday'. Maybe someone was worried about him for some reason. Once there, he behaves quite badly, especially towards the women working at Lövsta. A month later, he steals his employer's gun and fires it randomly. He flees to the woods, where he's finally overpowered by 25 Home Guardsmen and the police. Hilding is taken back to Lövsta.

24.8.48 Absconds during the day. Later in evening, visible in a haystack. As he was about to be brought back in, he slipped away. Later, the stable hill was searched, where he was found hidden deep in the hay. Refused to come out. When he was dragged forward, he screamed loudly and appeared confused. Was prevented at the last moment from throwing himself down from the hayloft.

25.8.48 Unable to work with his schoolmates, so must be left alone at Åsen.

10.48 Brought a schoolboy into the warehouse, tore off his clothes and beat him senselessly. [. . .] The boy screamed and when the other boys came, Hilding fled.

13.11.48 For no reason, other than as a 'joke', he punched Björklund in the mouth. Björklund was injured by the blow, i.e. cracked his lip. Hilding acts more and more impulsively and without forethought. Would like to have a knife to wave in front of his schoolmates' faces. Dangerous boy, should be isolated from society?

I see a clear shift in the record journal, a before and an after. After Hilding is transferred to the Lövsta Reformatory, he seems more stable. He's discharged to Perstorp on probation. All is going well; he's well liked by his family, neighbours and employers. Hilding behaves himself. But then, somewhere in the late spring or early summer of 1948, something happens. There is a shift from light to darkness, from calm to aggression.

The post about the rape Hilding was convicted of in 1952 is mentioned in Perstorp's Facebook group. A few people are unhappy attention has been drawn to this; they post critical comments in response, saying Hilding lived through hell on earth and atoned for his crime, let him rest in peace, people have done worse. One woman offers a different perspective. She writes that as a child she was told Hilding was also convicted of attempted murder. When I send her a message, she replies, and we speak on the phone.

I ask her if she ever met Hilding.

'Yes, oh yes,' she replies.

'What was your opinion of him as a person?'

'My mother was terrified of him. He had two very different sides to him.'

In the Perstorp group people recall how Hilding used to pop up unannounced at people's homes. While I read this, an odd noise starts coming from the baby monitor. Justus and I look up from our screens, listening. There's a rustling and squeaking. Suddenly, it sounds like a grown man whining and mumbling. I fly off the sofa, run up the stairs and into the bedroom where Vivi is sleeping peacefully in her bed.

My hands are shaking from nerves as the phone starts to ring. The Detective Inspector responds quickly.

'I could definitely imagine a sexual motive, even if there aren't those kinds of injuries, no physical signs,' he says. 'And I've talked to my colleagues about this, and one said right away: "This is sexual. No doubt in my mind." But there's still something clumsy about the murder. I don't think the perpetrator was a full-grown man, otherwise Birgitta would not have been able to run away. She made it 60 metres before he regained control of her. I'm thinking of that guy you described.'

'Hilding Samuelsson.'

'Hilding, yes . . .' The detective laughs. 'He's definitely a very good candidate. And I would guess this was a debut. It's a bit amateurish. But, in that case, Bengt was 14. It could very well . . . I mean, who's to say it wasn't him, really. There were some very convincing pieces of evidence: the shoes, the blood.'

We talk about Bengt for a while. I say he's certainly the right age, and the shoes and blood don't look good for him, even though the stains were probably old. But shouldn't he have gotten bloodier? And dirtier from carrying the stones? Besides, he doesn't seem to have been the violent type. The detective agrees.

'But, well . . . This Hilding. That's a damn good suspect. You asked what the perpetrator might have done after the crime, and I described it as a "cool off period". How, for those who serially commit violent and sexual crimes, the anxiety subsides, then comes back again. There's a build-up, and then you have to do it all over again. I get the idea that *if* this Hilding, who was later convicted of rape, was the one who murdered Birgitta, this was his debut.'

'There's another case that's very similar. A girl who was murdered at Hisingen two months after Birgitta,' I say.

'How far is that from Perstorp?'

'It's 220 kilometres. Her name was Harriet.' The detective's silent on the other end, so I continue. 'She was 8 years old, also murdered near a football field. The cause of death was blunt force trauma to the head, and the injuries were in the same location as Birgitta's: above the left eye, around the mouth on the left side, and in the back of the head. Harriet had an angular wound at the back of her head, and it reminded me of Birgitta's pointed injury. They found the murder weapon under the clubhouse − it was a rock.'

'Mmmmm.'

'But Harriet was raped. And I've been thinking about whether this could have been an escalation. If the same perpetrator was responsible.'

There's silence on the other end of the line. I'm about to say 'Hello?' when the Detective Inspector finally answers.

'Yes, that definitely sounds likely. Nowadays these two would have been connected immediately. The methods are absolutely similar. Geographically, they are a way apart, but . . . Same victim profile − a young girl − and the stone. I would definitely guess it was the same perpetrator.'

A weight seems to fall off my chest. Everyone else I've spoken to so far has downplayed these similarities. They think my imagination is running away with me.

'Because crimes like these against young girls are . . .' the detective continues.

'Very unusual,' I fill in.

'Yes. They are *extremely* unusual.'

By the time we hang up, we've been talking for almost an hour and a half. I lower my hands to the keyboard and notice they're still shaking.

HAPPIEST MOMENT OF MY LIFE, SAYS MOTHER OF PERSTORP YOUTH

'Justice has prevailed. We never gave up hope, and now our son is coming home. For us, it's a double vindication. We and our son have both been exonerated.'

The sun was shining from a clear autumn sky this Wednesday in the home of the Perstorp youth [. . .] Tears overwhelm the Perstorp mother as she attempts to explain her feelings in this moment of triumph.

'I've said it so many times, how I'd fight like a tigress for my son – and now we've won, I feel like a human being again.' [. . .]

The 14-year-old has now been dismissed from further suspicion in connection with the Perstorp drama. The Supreme Court has acquitted him of everything.

One evening I go for a walk, even though I really should go to bed. I've gone rather far along one of the paths in the nature reserve by the time I notice an email from the National Archives, received earlier in the day. It contains documents relating to the murder of Birgitta Stuge in Stavreviken, Medelpad, in June 1945. I read an article about it a while ago, but forgot I ordered the police investigation. I sit down on a rock and start to read. Some words flash out at me as if I placed a sheet of cut-outs on top of the text, as if I were using a secret code.

Birgitta
Bicycles
Lilies of the valley
9 years old
Seven thirty
Stream
Forest
Blows to the head

Birgitta Stuge, age 9, is out biking with her friend. They stop to pick lilies of the valley. A young man approaches them. He asks to borrow some tools to fix his bike. Birgitta goes to her bike to grab them. Then he attacks. Birgitta's friend manages to escape, but Birgitta is hunted down like an animal in the forest. She's found by a stream with serious injuries to her genital area and a severe blow to her head. The killer used a wrench, a gun and a knife.

I stand with my phone still in my hand and keep walking. I arrive at a place where the paths intersect. I stop and slowly look around. No one else is in sight. Terror bursts soundlessly in my chest as I realise that the figure of the murderer is timeless, a shadow that creeps always forward, an evil, pure as dark water that flows from deep beneath the earth and down our throats, a demon and a plague. It will never die, never be contained. If I keep searching, I will only find the same story repeated over and over and over. A space opens inside me, and I fall into it. I allow myself to be consumed. I crouch down and wait for the blow to the back of the head that never arrives.

The police investigation of the rape Hilding was convicted for in 1952 arrives in a flat, heavy archive box. I sit down at the kitchen table with the box, eagerly tear off the tape and toss it aside. Hilding was 19 when he stepped out of the woods onto a deserted dirt road and attacked a 35-year-old woman. It was a very snowy night. The police describe evidence on the ground of a fight near large piles of logs at the side of the road. There must have been shoe prints. I search for pictures of them, or anything written about footprints or Hilding's shoes in the investigation, but there's nothing. The disappointment is sharp.

My phone is about to die so I get up to plug it in, running a hand over Sam's thick hair. He doesn't look up. I turn on the lamp above the kitchen table; the already warm light seems somehow warmer against the backdrop of the blue outside. At the bottom of the pile, I find a mental assessment of Hilding. The doctor writes that Hilding didn't like being examined by a woman. Childishly, arms crossed over his chest, he sits across from her curtly answering her questions. In the orphanage records, they only wrote *about* him. This is the first time I hear his voice in the text. I grab a pencil and briefly jot down the doctor's description of Hilding as a person:

> Unable to tell right from wrong
> Unable to control himself
> Like a man possessed
> Difficult to determine if he's hallucinating, but there are many
> indications as such

298

Indifferent to everything except his motorcycle, including family
Combination of emotional coldness and impulsivity
Above-average IQ
Psychopath of the emotional type
Sadistically brutal and dangerous

A memory flashes into my mind. I was the same age as Hilding, sitting opposite a female doctor. I had just dropped out of high school for the second time, and they sent me to a psychologist to be evaluated. Very reluctantly, I sat down in the chair across from her. I must have been rude. I didn't want to be there. I remember her asking me how I looked at time. I replied that time, well, you can look at it in different ways. Like a circle. Or a line. Or a ball of yarn. She wasn't satisfied by my answer. We started arguing, and she insisted on a more concrete answer.

How many times did Hilding and this doctor meet? Those were strong words she used, 'sadistically brutal and dangerous'. What prompted them?

I think of the letter that was at the top of the pile of mail from the public. It's written in blue ink and riddled with typos. It says that two boys rode the train from Perstorp to Gothenburg the same evening the murder was committed. *They had murder on their conscience.* The letter is dated 21 August 1948. *I'm leaving from Gothenburg tonight so you'll never catch me.* It took me two years to consider that this letter might have been placed on top for a reason. That was when I started reading the investigation into Harriet's murder. I remembered those lines, about the boys going to Gothenburg. It seemed strangely specific. If someone was just making it up, why Gothenburg? It could be a coincidence, but the letter is the only thing that links the locations of Birgitta's and Harriet's murders. I lie awake wondering if Hilding might have written it. His medical records include a letter he wrote to the Lövsta Reformatory. I read it over and over again, comparing the handwriting with the letter sent to the police.

At the time the letter the police received was written, Hilding was 15 going on 16. The second letter was written when he was 16 and had gone to sea. Now and then, I think I see some similarities in the handwriting, but I lean towards not. Hilding's letter has rounder penmanship, while the handwriting in the letter to the police is somewhat pinched.

'You know,' says the Detective Inspector when I call him one morning, 'you could check those letters for fingerprints.'

'Do you mean it? Could they still be there after all this time?'

'Yes, it's quite possible.'

I get excited and my thoughts drift in that direction, but I quickly pull back.

'But, is it possible to do without damaging the original material?'

'Well, they'd probably end up with some stains on them.'

I sigh deeply.

'I doubt the archive would approve of that.'

I wake up to the door closing; Justus just got up with Vivi. I look at the time. It's 4:48am. I was in the middle of a dream. As I lay back down in the same position as before, I start to remember it. Young men were running around me, or were they wolves? They had their shining teeth bared, foaming at the mouth, their throats vibrating with growls. Eyes black as onyx with rage. I recognised one of them and froze in fear as he stared at me. Now I realise why: he was the boy I dreamed about several months ago. Sam's friend, who lunged at me and tried to claw his way into my stomach. 'Let me in! Let me in!' he shouted. I haven't been able to let go of that dream.

I feel cold. Is it him? Am I dreaming about the killer? Is he haunting me? I swallow hard and sit up. Turn my phone's flashlight on and slowly shine it around the room. The sharp white light reveals an open closet, a laundry basket, Vivi's bed. I want to shine it behind the canopy of Vivi's bed just to make sure, but that feels like giving in somehow.

Sometimes I wonder if I am going mad. Between sunset and sunrise, I enter a symbolic realm that tells of dark forces unleashed upon the world. The dream boy is a demon trying to enter me. The same demon is responsible for Birgitta and Harriet's deaths, which is why this pattern repeats itself – a rock to the left temple, left jaw, the back of the head.

But it doesn't matter whether or not you believe in these other-worldly explanations. The question is: how many wounded, angry wolves were on the loose in Perstorp and Lundby in the spring and summer of 1948? The killer's name might be one I've never even read.

On a hot summer day, I'm in the Old Town with Sam. I've decided we need to hang out more, just the two of us. He takes my hand as we walk over the cobblestone streets.

'Should we go in there?' I say, pointing to the City Mission.

'What is it?'

'It's like a flea market.'

He adores flea markets, because he adores old things. His eyes light up, and he jumps a little. While he examines all the old uniforms that adorn the mannequins inside, I dig through the jewellery. I throw enamelled leopards and dangling wooden earrings aside like Moses parting the sea. At the bottom glitters a rhinestone eight. It's a brooch and costs 40 kronor. I buy it.

On the subway, in the middle of Sam's lecture on Telefonia, an archivist from the National Archives in Gothenburg calls.

'I can see you've ordered copies of the investigation into the murder of Harriet Schelin again,' he says.

'Yes,' I say, 'I forgot to download the files before they expired. But I was also hoping there might be more. According to the press, there should be photos of the crime scene and forensic examinations.'

'That's right,' says the archivist, 'there's definitely more. That's why I'm calling. What we sent you last time was an excerpt. The entire investigation is about five hundred pages long.'

'Oh.'

'It's probably best if you come down to Gothenburg.'

I leave home early to catch the train. As it rolls through town I see something written on the underside of a bridge. *You are the disease, we are the symptom.* What creates these monsters? Violence begets violence begets violence. Some victims of violence turn inward, harming only themselves. Others become beasts, teeth bared and claws out. Evil is like a chain that runs backwards through time. Mud and fog obscure our view, making it impossible to see where it begins.

It's half past eleven when the train rolls into Gothenburg. I decide to head straight to the archives. The archivists have laid out my material in a separate room behind the counter. 'Please keep the door closed,' they tell me. 'Some of those pictures are quite explicit.'

I look away while taking pictures with my phone, quickly, one page at a time. Every time I turn a page, I feel apprehensive. I don't know when the pictures will arrive. The room's getting hotter and hotter. I sense something crawling near my temples, but when I put my hand there it's just drops of sweat. Even though the air is quite still, something rustles inside the radiator to my left. Every time I look, it falls silent. When an archivist knocks to announce they're closing, I still haven't arrived at the explicit photos, but I've managed to take pictures of quite a bit, about three hundred pages.

By the time I arrive at the hotel I'm out of breath and flushed red. My room number is 261, on the second floor. Once there, I take off my sweaty clothes and lay in the middle of the bed, panting. I open my pictures app — I might as well start reading what I managed to photograph. But there aren't many pictures. It doesn't make sense. I look at the time stamp on the pictures. In the beginning, I averaged eight per minute. Between 12:14 and 12:25 there are no pictures, even though I know I didn't take a break. Between 12:26 and 12:30 there's another gap. After that, there's about one frame per minute, with gaps in between.

I roll over onto my back. Thunder is close by. *It's Harriet*, I think. *Maybe she doesn't want me to see.*

I read the pages that haven't disappeared. One of them is a letter addressed to the defence attorney of the man convicted of Harriet's murder. The lawyer forwarded the letter to the police because he wants them to investigate Harriet's moral character, which, according to him, 'despite her young age reportedly left much to be desired'. The anonymous letter reads as follows.

Dear Sir,

[. . .] Man to man, it is truly regrettable that an otherwise irreproachable worker came to lose his head over this little hooligan, this whore, to speak plainly. [. . .] The ridiculous sainthood and stupid nonsense, that the press poured over her person and death and funeral are laughable for anyone who knows Lundby and knows the girl and her so-called home. [. . .] In this case, our community has been relieved of a particularly unpleasant developing specimen.

It's regrettable that society should have to lose such a splendid worker, sacrificed for a bitch, whose mother should be the one receiving punishment. [. . .]

The whole neighbourhood shares this opinion. This message is coming from hundreds, who are hereby represented.

Respectfully,
A newspaper reader, disgusted by the pathetic hagiography the press is performing.

Did people really think this way? I see Harriet's face before me. What had she been through? Is the fact that Harriet was considered a 'bitch' and a 'whore' the reason no one seems to remember her murder today? That, and because she came from a working-class family? The thought that this lawyer didn't just crumple up the letter and throw it away makes my head spin with disbelief. That the police even received it, gave it enough importance to preserve it for posterity, feels insane. Perhaps because it was a different time, but people have always been people, right? An 8-year-old is still an 8-year-old. I see Harriet in front of me, her tiny shoulders weighed down by something she can't possibly understand and hasn't asked for or earned – contempt for her class and gender.

The next day, after photographing the entire investigation on my now working phone, I have time to spare before the train leaves. I head out to Lundby. On the way, I read the investigation. Arne Persson, the welder convicted of Harriet's murder, changes his story several times. He finally confesses that he raped and murdered Harriet after chasing into her in the clubhouse. She used to go there to use the bathroom, talk to the old men and ask for change. Arne was the club caretaker and used to get angry at the kids running around there. 'Get out of here, or I'll kill you,' he'd growl. When Arne later retracts his confession, no one believes him. And he is the most likely culprit. However, one detail makes me hesitate – he was an avid reader. He read everything he came across, including several newspapers a day. How much could he have picked up from them? And how leading were the police's questions? It's not clear from the investigation if Arne led the police to the murder weapon – the stone beneath the clubhouse – or if the police found it. I don't feel totally convinced it really was him. *Guilty beyond a reasonable doubt*, as they say. I wouldn't describe it that way.

Harriet rests near Lundby's new church. Rights to the burial plot have returned to the grantor, but I know the grave number and I start searching. The ground is covered with yellow leaves, and dark clouds gather above the trees. At the site of Harriet's grave, there now stands a stone bearing two other names. They died in the 1990s. I wonder what their relatives would think if they knew their ancestors had been lain on top of a raped and murdered 8-year-old. No one seems to have been here for a long time; there are no flowers or candles. A sarcophagus-like block lies in front of the headstone. I sit on its edge, and the rain starts to fall. I pick up a handful of gravel from the neighbouring grave. I intend to write only an H, but keep going with the rest of her name. After I leave, I hope someone stops and wonders who Harriet was.

When I finally arrived at the pictures of Harriet's body in the archive, I exclaimed 'Oh God.' I felt like throwing up. I flipped past quickly, but I can't seem to rid myself of them. Especially one. I'm on the train now, but I can still see it in front of me. I dig into my bag for a sedative. All I have is promethazine, and I take two. I can see that picture – a gaping abyss, a black hole, the gateway to hell – all the way home. I absorb it, and when I hug Sam on the sofa and ask how everything went, I'm filled with it, and when I lie down next to Vivi, who just woke up, I'm swallowed by it. She can't get back to sleep. She must sense the field of darkness vibrating around me.

At five o'clock I wake up, confused, teeth unbrushed. My contacts have dried up in my eyes so I go to take them out. In the darkness of the bathroom, I sink down onto cold tile and cry. In three weeks, Vivi will start preschool, and Sam elementary school. How will I protect them? Before I went to Gothenburg, I felt better than I had in a long time; I felt proud and hopeful. I thought maybe I was close to a solution, an ending. But I know now that it just keeps going. The questions I have about the murder of Harriet, about Arne's guilt or innocence, are too numerous. And what did Hilding do in the time before and after Birgitta's murder? Both Birgitta and Harriet were murdered at football fields; could that really be a coincidence? Could someone whose name never even appeared in either investigation be guilty of both? A completely unknown perpetrator who has flown under the radar all these years? I'm being swallowed by the darkness. I don't want to do this anymore.

I'm standing behind Hilding, who is bent over the railing in the dark. The ship he's assigned to is called the *Marianne Bratt* – Bratt as in Margit's maiden name. When Hilding was boarding, he turned back and caught sight of his teacher from the Lövsta Reformatory waving from atop the cobblestones in the harbour. Hilding's eyes had filled with tears. It's the only straw for me to grab on to, the only detail that attests to even an ounce of softness left inside him. Now his eyes are shining coldly as he watches the last crane disappear behind the horizon. The air is heavy with water and salt. It blows up from the sea below like a very fine, misdirected rain.

The dim light from the boat is reflected in thousands of tiny drops on the coarse wool of Hilding's jacket. I raise my hand and hold it in the air behind his neck. I can see the hairs on the back of his neck stand up, but he remains completely still as I gently place it against his skin. I stand next to him and lean forward to see his face. He's only 16 years old, but looks older. His face radiates either sadness or defiance, depending on who's looking.

I whisper question after question into his ear; I stay there until he heads into his cabin and pulls the rough blanket over his head. After he falls asleep, I enter his dreams. He laughs coldly at me. When I stubbornly continue, he jerks forward, with menace in his black eyes. But I force myself closer and closer. I go so close our pupils meet. The darkness inside mine presses against the darkness in his. His knees give way; finally he lies down. The defiance, the violence, the sadness and the anger drain out of him until it's an enormous sea of tar. Now he's as soft and malleable as clay. I cup my hands and place them on his shoulders. I press them together. They turn thin and weak.

When the night is over, a child is lying there. I grab him under his armpits and lift him onto my lap. I rock him, sing into his hair. His head becomes heavy. His arms turn limp. Slowly I lay him down again. His cheeks are rosy, and his mouth falls open in sleep. I pull up the covers, lean over him and put my hand to his cheek. Then I gently lift it away.

Just as I've placed a piece of bread in Vivi's hand and raised my cup for a first sip of coffee, I hear Sam getting up. From that moment on, I float as helplessly as a bark boat on a stormy sea through the rest of my morning. After breakfast, I carefully dry Vivi's hands and cheeks, take off her pyjamas and put on the clothes I laid out last night: a ribbed, linden-green onesie, cocoa-brown ribbed tights with suspenders, a small velvet jacket in the same colour, and a leopard-print collar. Sam chooses his own clothes: dark blue pants and a small-chequered shirt. I remember exactly what I wore on my first day of school: a raspberry-pink skirt in thick, soft cotton and a white knitted cotton sweater with embroidered roses. Justus and Sam head to the subway ahead of us.

'Bye, honey!' I shout to Sam from the hall, and to Justus: 'Remember to take pictures.'

There's something off with Vivi this morning; maybe she senses something, knows everything will be different now.

'It's okay,' I assure her. 'Mummy's here.'

We make our way through torrential rain to the subway. Vivi doesn't say a word. Once we get to the platform my mouth twitches, I make up my mind. I take out the baby carrier, fasten it around my waist, pry Vivi out through the hatch of the pushchair's rain cover. She bounces her legs.

'Up!' she shouts. 'Up!'

I smooth the carrier over her back and fasten the buckle behind my neck. She puts her head against my sternum and strokes my cheek.

'Pat Mummy.'

The subway arrives, and we climb on. I lock the pushchair wheels and stroke Vivi's back with both my hands, kiss her head, her forehead, her cheeks. This is the last time she'll be just a baby. Today she's becoming a pre-schooler.

When Sam gets home from school, I have lunch ready on the table. Apparently, he was already served lunch, but he eats again anyway.

'If he's had two big meals today, maybe we should just make cinnamon toast for dinner?' I say to Justus.

We both tilt our heads, as if thinking it over.

'What's that?' Sam says, putting down his fork.

'Well, it's like pancakes, but with bread. You put sugar and cinnamon on it.'

His eyes widen, he drops his fork and it clatters against his plate.

'Yes!' Sam says. Then he stops. 'Wait a minute, are you joking?'

He's lost both of his front teeth in the last week. His canines look like little vampire teeth. It's so cute it makes me cringe inside. Justus and I laugh.

'No, we would never do that.'

Sam stands up suddenly and picks up his plate, carries it over to the sink. He's never done that before.

'Mum,' he says and I look up.

He's standing on the rag rug, turned halfway away from me. I stand up and clear my own plate.

'Yes?' I say.

He turns to me.

'I *love you*.'

315

Silently on tiptoes, the girls steal through the darkened apartment like a coiling snake in a long line. Their bright skirts bob, their big bows droop. They walk over the rugs and creep up the stairs. In his bedroom, the boy is asleep, fencing with his arm.

'Mum, they're coming now. Mum, they're here,' he mumbles, but no one hears him.

The girls pass by his door and step through the next. They smile at the baby girl sleeping by the wall, the curly hair on the nape of her neck, her cheeks rosy from sleep. Her father's reassuringly heavy arm is stretched across her; her tiny hand rests lightly on his. The girls walk to the bed on the other side of the room. A woman lies sleeping there with her face towards the wall. Her dark hair is gathered in a tangled braid, which winds like a river across her pillow. Her breathing is deep and slow. The first girl sits down slowly on the edge of the bed, while the others follow, folding into each other until they are a singular figure that weighs down the mattress. The girl dangles her legs over the edge, her upper body turned toward the sleeping woman, who sighs heavily now.

The girl sits there for a long time, staring at the rounded shoulders as they rise and fall in time with her breathing. When the woman is completely motionless, deep in sleep, the girl leans slowly over her. She cups a hand around the woman's ear. The woman's eyes open wide in terror. She stares into the darkness. The woman's mouth opens, but no sound comes out. The girls unfold again without a sound. The bed creaks as their weight disappears. The door slides open, and the line of girls disappears out through it, as silently as they arrived.

Afterword

Less than a month before this book goes to print, I receive an email from the National Archives in Lund. It is from an archivist who found a new file regarding Birgitta's case, one I haven't read. I feel almost faint when I read it. Could it be the so-called slush – what they sorted out of the police investigation as unimportant when they were deciding on a prime suspect? Will it turn this book upside down?

I read the documents eagerly. I'm searching for a name – Hilding. His name isn't there, but among those papers I do find a newspaper clipping about him. The headline reads: *Volunteers Hunted Young Desperado*. The investigators apparently attached no importance to it. However, they did take an interest in several other people, most of them after the trial of Bengt.

Maybe you, my readers, are disappointed there's no solution. That this isn't a whodunnit with a clear ending. Perhaps you wonder if I think I know who murdered Birgitta? The answer is no.

The question I've asked myself every day since I read that first article about the murder is: who did it? Who ran Birgittta into the ditch on that May evening, some seventy years ago? My suspicions have fallen on several different people, but lately, I've been thinking maybe the name isn't what matters. What matters is building a society that prevents children from growing up to become dangerous people.

I believe no human is born evil. Safe and happy people don't commit murder. The person I've chosen to call Hilding Samuelsson is one example of a person who received neither the love nor the care every child is entitled to, and who apparently grew up to be a dangerous man. But what I won't say is: he did it. I don't know who committed the murder.

An upbringing like Hilding's, insecure and troubled, can be a factor in going on to commit violence. But, of course, not everyone who grows up in those conditions turns out dangerous. Nature versus nurture – that's a discussion I'll leave to the experts.

I've written this story the way I imagined reality, based on the closest I could get to the source material. And the material is enormous – police investigations, court hearings, newspaper articles, medical records and interviews. It has steered this ship. Almost everything that takes place in this text in the past is based on events and dialogue from that time; I've used many words that appeared in police and court interviews and written many lines based on them.

However, even the richest source material can't tell us the whole truth, and there are many gaps. I've tried to fill them in to the best of my ability, and with empathy. Settings I don't know, such as people's homes, I've imagined based on descriptions and pictures of similar settings of the time. Sometimes I've given someone the emotions I think I would have felt in their situation. I've taken the liberty of entering other people's minds. I've done this to humanise the people I'm writing about, to give them the voice they lack in the source material.

Out of concern for those affected and their survivors, I changed the names of every person who played no official role in the investigations. This includes family members, neighbours and acquaintances who ended up in the middle of a murder investigation without the protection a professional title provides. As for the people who held official roles, I've used what they themselves told the press or other officials, or wrote. Some of it is not entirely flattering. But I ask readers to take into account that they lived in a different time, and also that a completely fair picture is impossible, because you can never show every aspect of a person.

Acknowledgements

My first and most heartfelt thanks goes to Birgitta's older brother, Karl Sivander. If you had said no that first time, there would be no book. You've been so generous with your thoughts, memories and anecdotes, and I cannot find the words to thank you enough. Not only have I gained a good friend, but with your help I came to know some of the most important people in this story, even though they're no longer with us. I hope you feel I've done you, your sister and your family justice.

This book was written during the best time in my life, even though it may not always seem like it. They say your total quota of happiness doesn't change after you have children, but the peaks get higher, and the valleys lower. My highs have been so breathtakingly high, that I would never say no to the lows. Sam and Vivi, you are everything to me. Sorry for being absent so often. I love you more than the universe is big. And Justus, you too. Thank you for all your patience while I've been writing, for never questioning me, for reading and commenting over and over, and for listening to me when I've interrupted whatever we're doing to discuss details from the investigations. Thank you also to my family and friends: Mimmi, for your endless support and taking me to Perstorp. Rannveig, child and adolescent psychiatrist, for not only being one of my best friends, but also sharing your expertise with me so generously. Idha, for letting me stay with you in Lund, and for going to the archive in my place. Thank you Lone and Sigrid for your friendship. And Erika Stark, who's not just a friend but also a writer – you've made this a much less lonely job.

Many thanks to Ola and Hanna, who read the medical records through the eyes of psychologists and told me what they saw there. Thank you Åsa Edergren for your surgical experience in interpreting the autopsy reports. Thanks to all the archivists who located, copied and sent me material. A thousand thanks to homicide detective Jan Ullén, and to the anonymous person whom I call the Detective Inspector, whose expertise was worth its weight in gold – both of you are such lovely people. Thanks to everyone who was willing to speak to me about Perstorp, about the murder and about that time period. Thank you to Shida Shahabi, Amason, Dolce, Anna von Hausswolff, Nino Rota and Erik Satie, who, unknowingly, were essential to the creation of this book. Thanks to my publisher, Johanna Haegerström, for taking this on and believing in it as a book. It's felt so safe to have you only the touch of a button and a subway station away. And thank you to my editor, Rachel Åkerstedt, who received a rough stone and helped me chisel, grind and polish it.

Thank you to my agent, Astri von Arbin Ahlander, for sending my book into the world; to Elizabeth Clark Wessel who translated this book into English; and to my UK publisher, Sarah Braybrooke.

Bengt was contacted by letter on several occasions, but did not respond.

I'm sorry, Perstorp.

Linda Segtnan, Kärrtorp, May 2022

In memory of Birgitta Sivander

Sources

Unpublished Source Material

National Archives in Lund
The Malmö City Police archives
Police investigation into the murder of Inger Birgitta Sivander, 1948

Västra Göinge district court archives
Documents in criminal cases, 1952
Correctional institution in Kristianstad's archives, prison rolls, 1952

Norra Åsbo district court archives
Trial documents, 1948
Public prosecutor of Riseberga's archive of criminal case diaries

National Archives in Gothenburg
Gothenburg City Hall court
Police investigation, court documents and verdict concerning the murder of Anita Harriet Schelin, 1948

Central seamen's register archives
The Seamen's House in Kristianstad, register of shipmasters and seamen, 1949–1957

Regional archive in Skåne
Råbylund home, journals, 1941–1944

National Archives in Uppsala
Lövsta Reformatory, records, 1940–1982

Stockholm City Archives
Society Pro Patria, patient records, 1938

Published Source Material

Dagens Nyheter
1948-05-09
1948-05-12
1948-07-05
1948-07-06
1948-07-07
1948-07-08
1948-07-09
1948-07-11
1948-07-13
1948-07-15
1948-07-23
1948-07-25
1948-07-27

Expressen
1948-07-17
1948-10-06

Stockholms-Tidningen
1948-05-10

Aftonbladet
1948-07-04

Arbetet
1948-07-06

Works Cited

p. 13 Edith Södergran: 'Skogsdunkel', *Dikter*, Schildt, 1916

p. 60 Maria Gripe: *Agnes Cecilia: En sällsam historia*, Bonniers juniorförlag, 1981

p. 120 Anna Bergström: 'Blommornas bön', *Sångkurs för skolan*, 1923

p. 120 Psalm 283

p. 129 from Gustaf Fröding: 'Ormens sång', 1914

p. 253 Eva Neander: 'Död idyll', *Död idyll*, Bonniers, 1947

p. 282 Otto Lindwall: 'Konvaljens avsked', 1905

Images

p. vi Linda Segtnan/Anna Torsteinsrud, map

p. 3 Birgitta Sivander, private photo

p. 168 Shoes and shoe prints, from the investigation into the murder of Birgitta Sivander

p. 322 Birgitta Sivander, private photo

All other photos Linda Segtnan